MW01625784

Grandi Musei per Piccoli Visitatori

1. The Uffizi Gallery in Florence

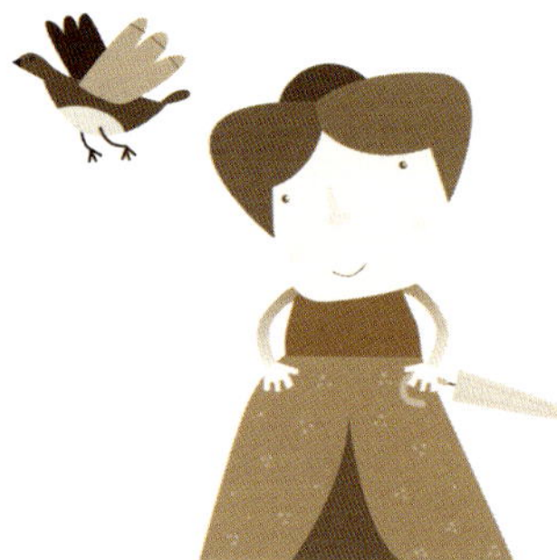

ISBN 88-8347-160-1

A publication by
s i l l a b e s.r.l.
Livorno
www.sillabe.it
info@sillabe.it

managing editor: Maddalena Paola Winspeare
editing: Giulia Bastianelli
translation: Anthony Cafazzo

project by:
Lungarno editore s.r.l., Firenze
redazione@lungarnoeditore.it

text by: *Brenda Bimbi, M. Lisa Guarducci*

lay-out and drawings:
Francesca D'Alfonso

reproduction rights: *Archivio Sillabe: P. Nannoni; Rabatti e Domingie Photography; Archivio Museo di Casa Buonarroti*

the Gallery of the Accademia in Florence

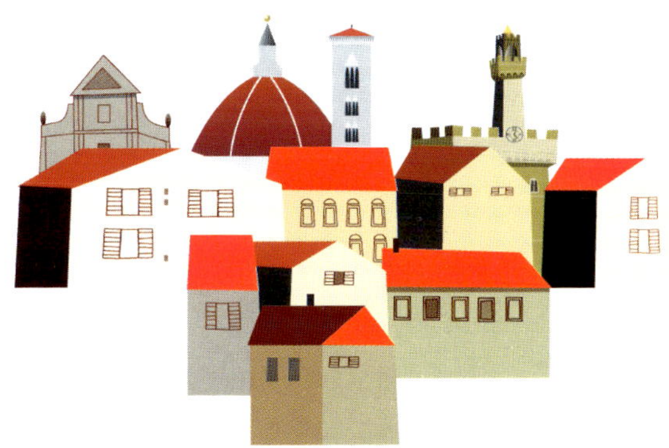

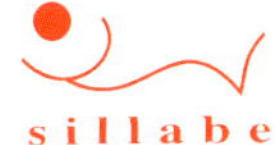

sillabe

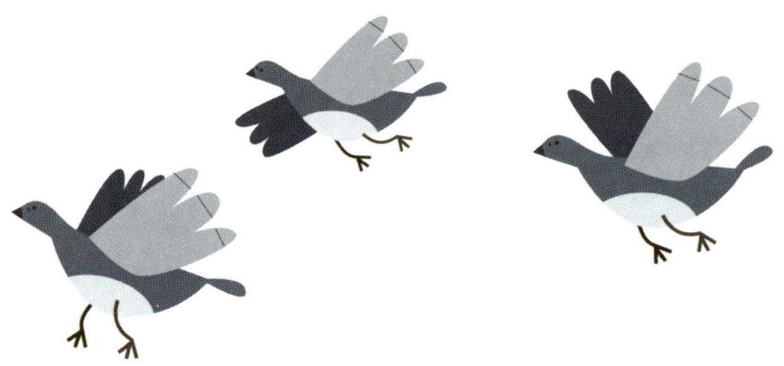

"Extra! Extra! Read all about it! *Giant* to be moved to the Academy today! Read all about it!"

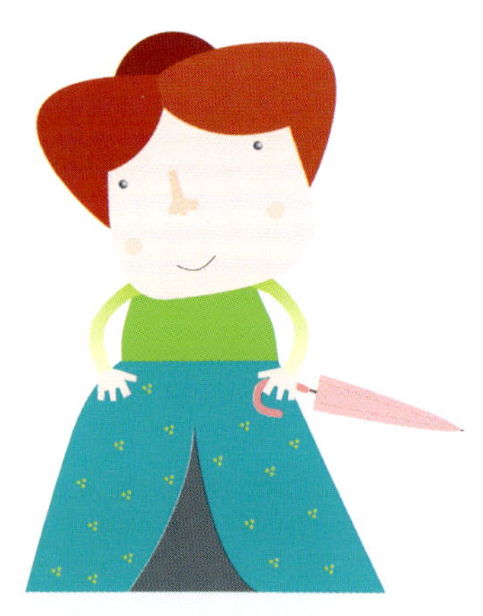

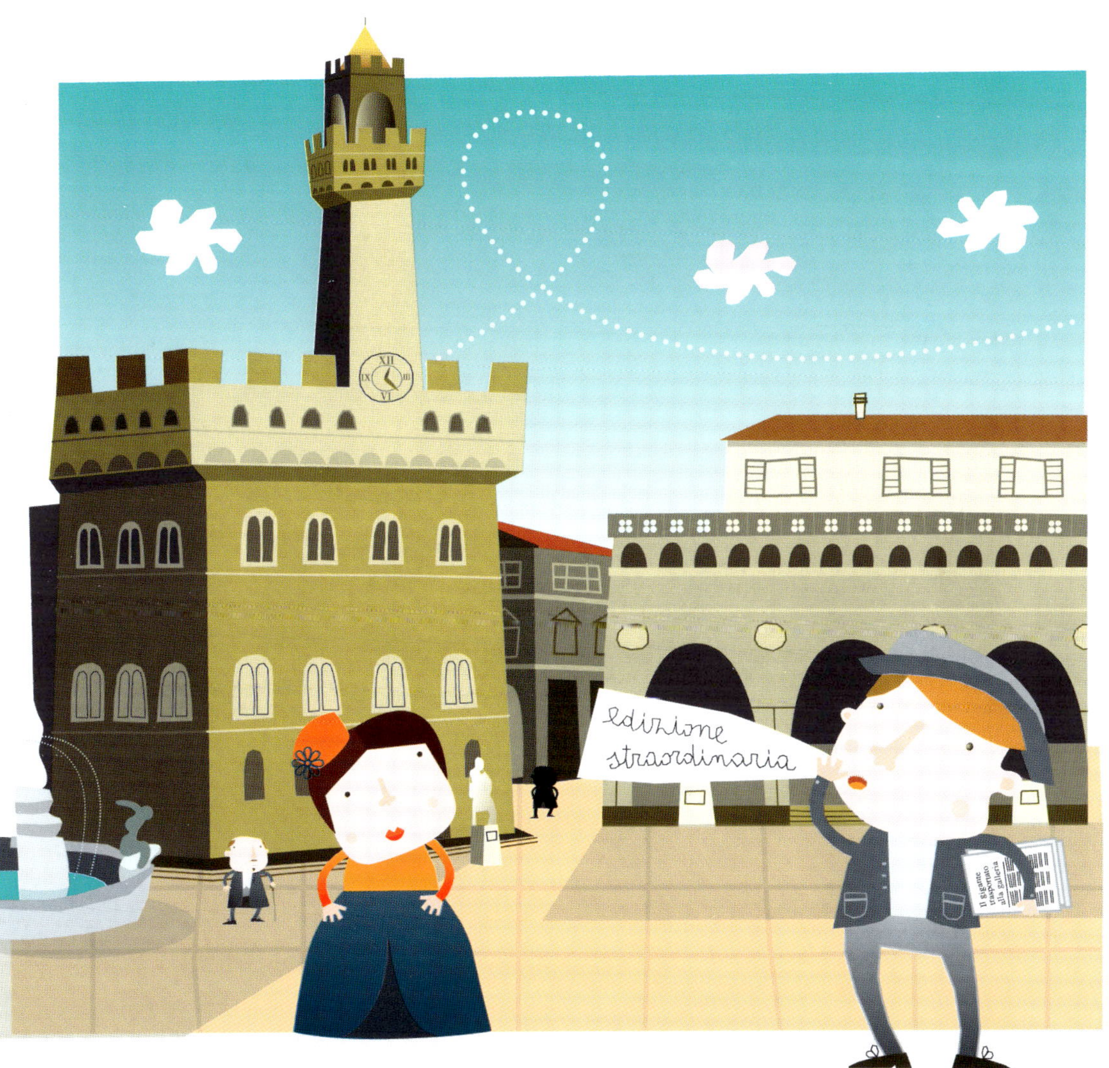

Edizione straordinaria
Il gigante trasportato alla galleria

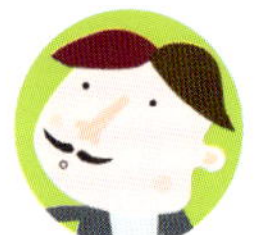 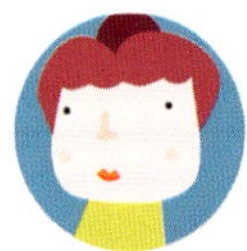 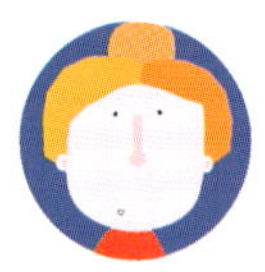 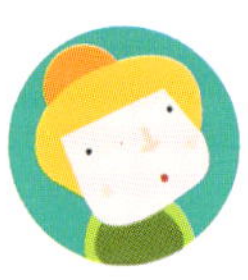 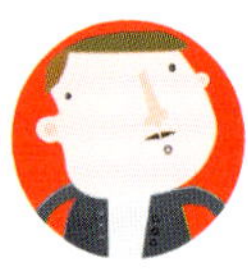  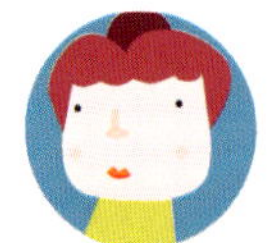

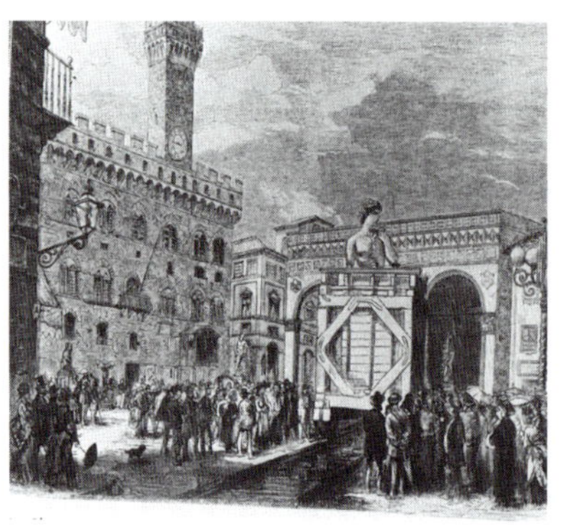

Transferring Michelangelo's David, from "Nuova Illustrazione Universale", 1874

It was 1873, and that morning, July 31, the whole city of Florence held its breath as its most famous statue, *David*, was moved from Piazza della Signoria, where it had always stood, to the recently opened Museum of the Accademia, in the city quarter of San Marco.

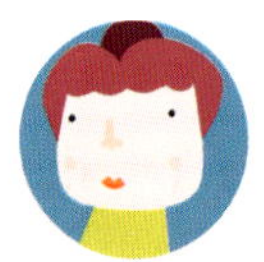 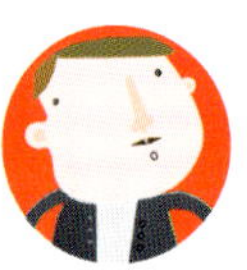 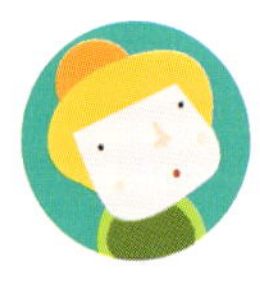  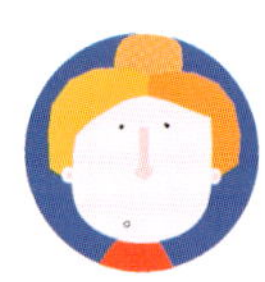 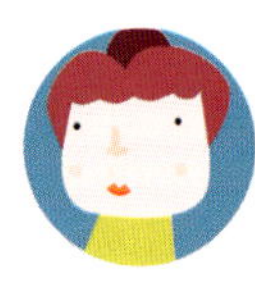 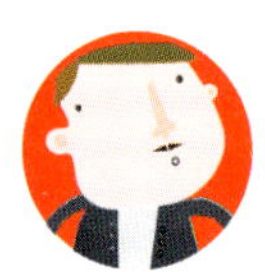

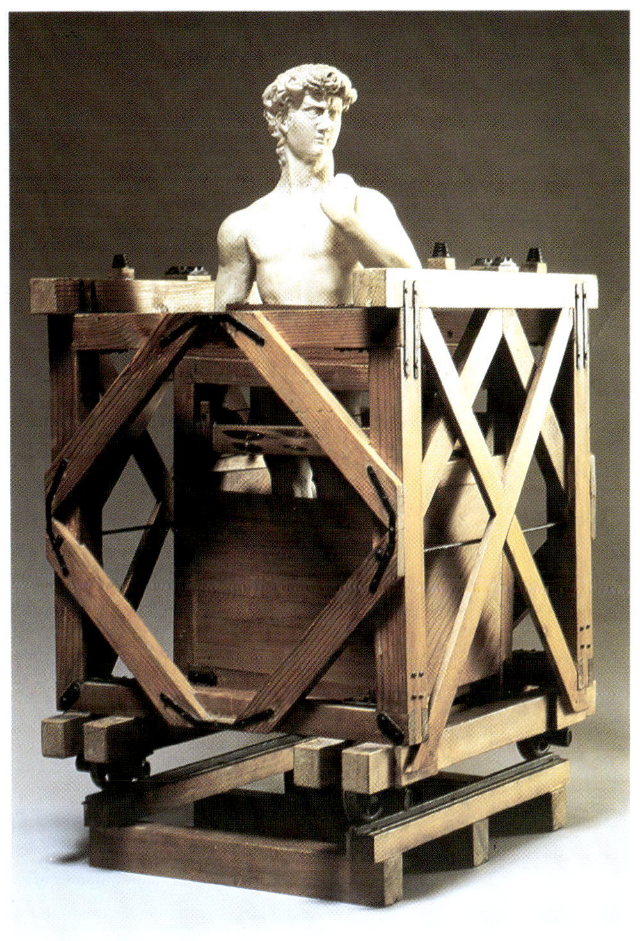

Model of the wagon used to transport *David* from Piazza della Signoria to the Gallery of the Accademia, 1873, Florence, Museo di Casa Buonarroti

In order to transport the *Giant,* the Florentines had built a complicated framework that rolled along rails. For the people of Florence, this was a great occasion, and large crowds gathered along the route were the statue would pass. It took five days to complete the move: only on August 4 did *David* arrive at its new museum.

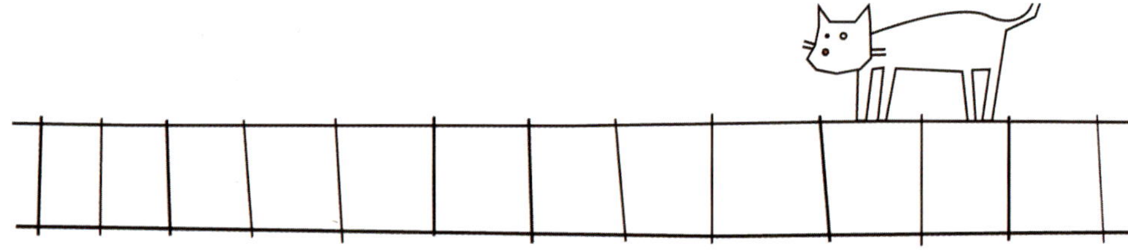

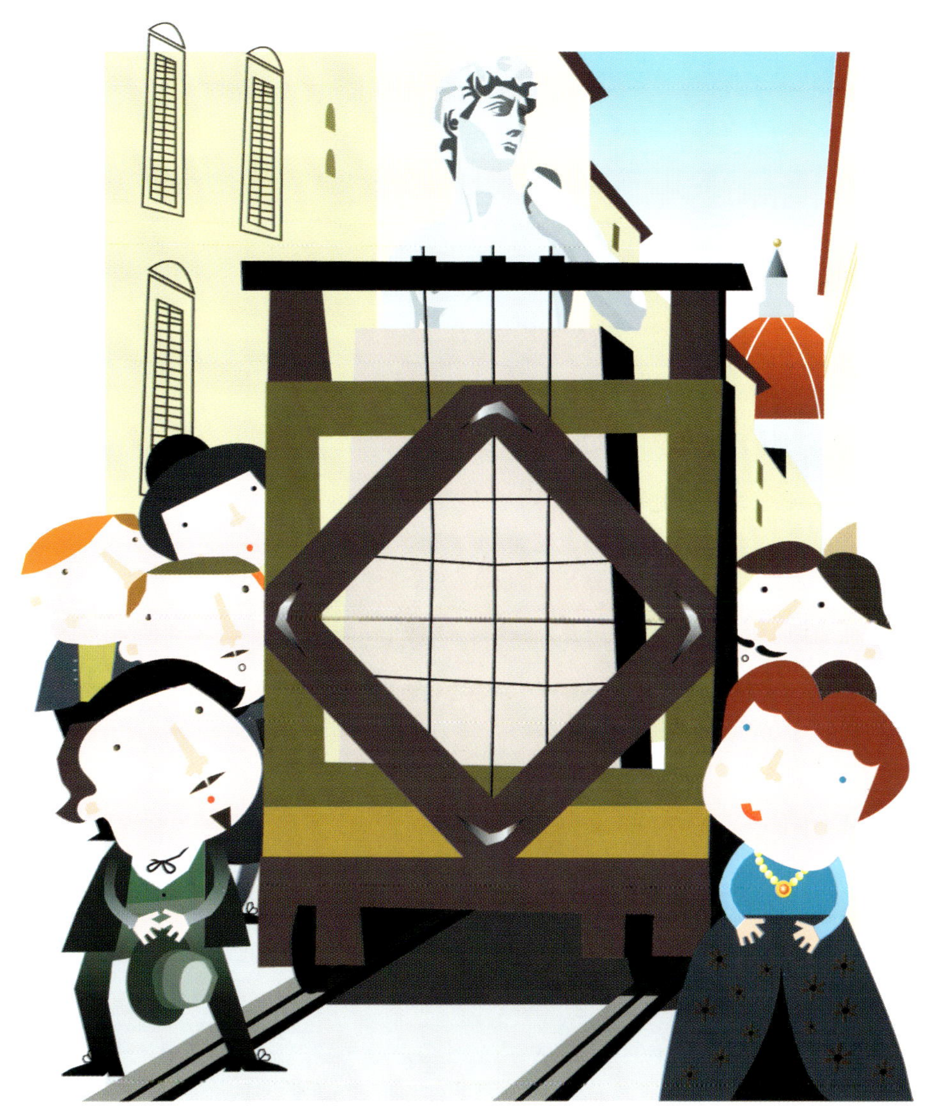

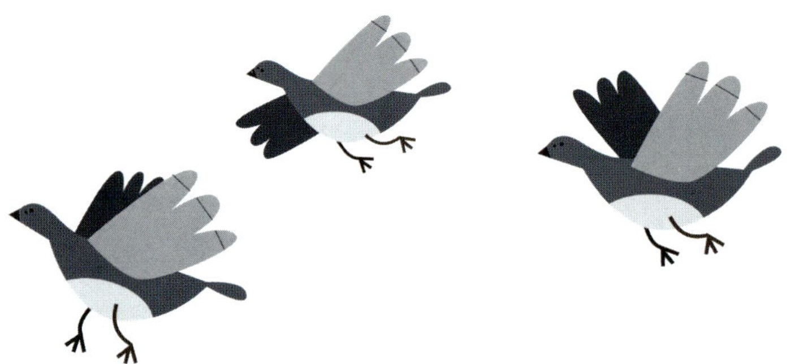

From Piazza della Signoria, the famous sculpture was drawn along the crowded, bustling streets of the old quarter of San Marco. Important, age-old religious buildings lined the way: the churches of San Marco and Santissima Annunziata, schools, theatres and the Accademia delle Belle Arti, that is, the Academy of Fine Arts, where young artists gathered and studied.

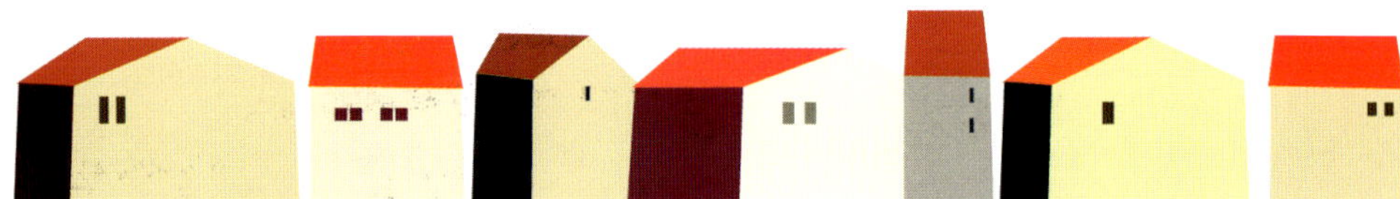

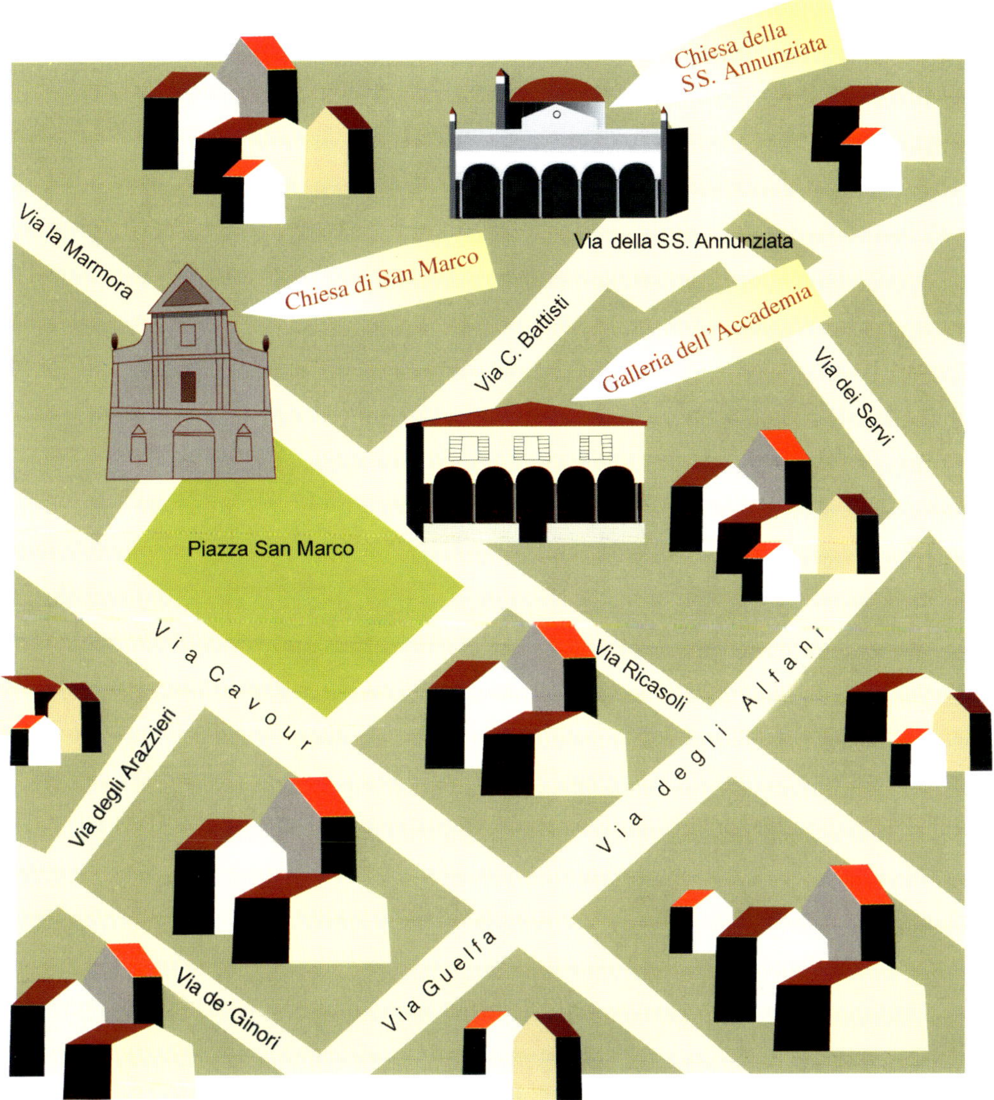
Chiesa della SS. Annunziata
Via della SS. Annunziata
Via la Marmora
Chiesa di San Marco
Via C. Battisti
Galleria dell' Accademia
Via dei Servi
Piazza San Marco
Via Cavour
Via Ricasoli
Via degli Alfani
Via degli Arazzieri
Via de' Ginori
Via Guelfa

Many centuries earlier, during the Middle Ages, this area had been home to the monastery of San Matteo and convent of San Niccolò di Cafaggio, named for the many beech trees (*faggio*), hedges and canals that used to be found here. San Matteo also used to be a hospital, whose entrance in the square of San Marco was through a loggia.

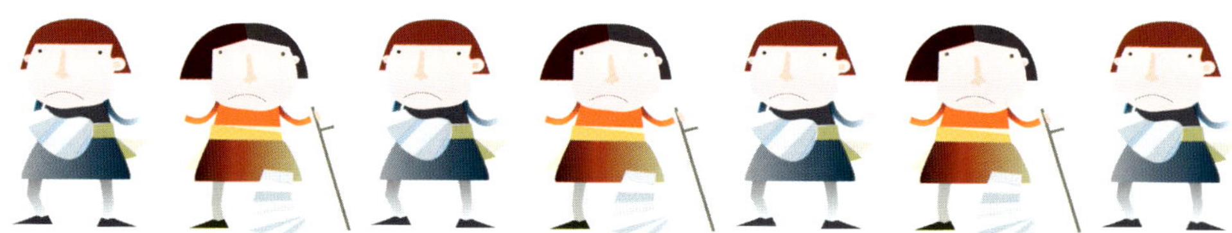

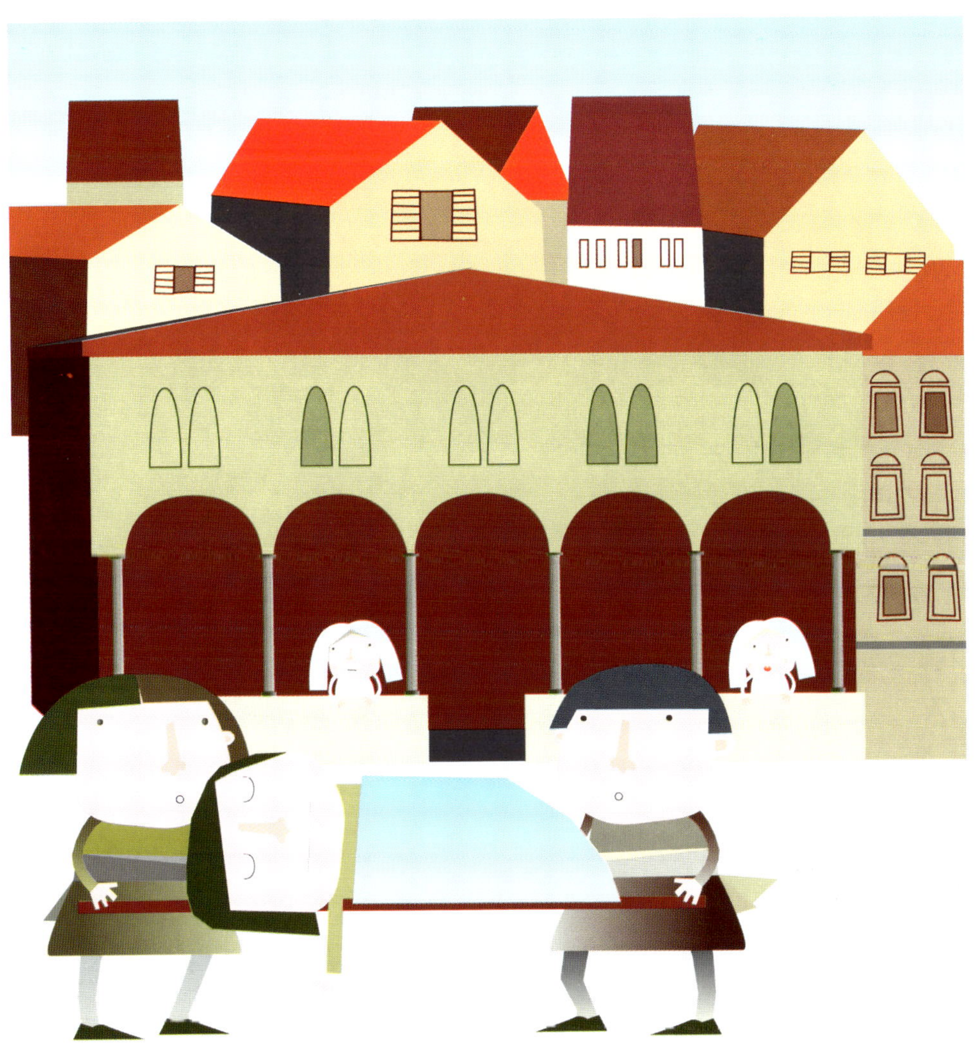

In the 18th century the Lorraine Grand Duke, Pietro Leopoldo, decided to make this area Florence's *Citadel of Art*. So, the Accademia delle Belle Arti, the Opificio delle Pietre Dure and the Conservatory of Music were all established here in the space of a few years.

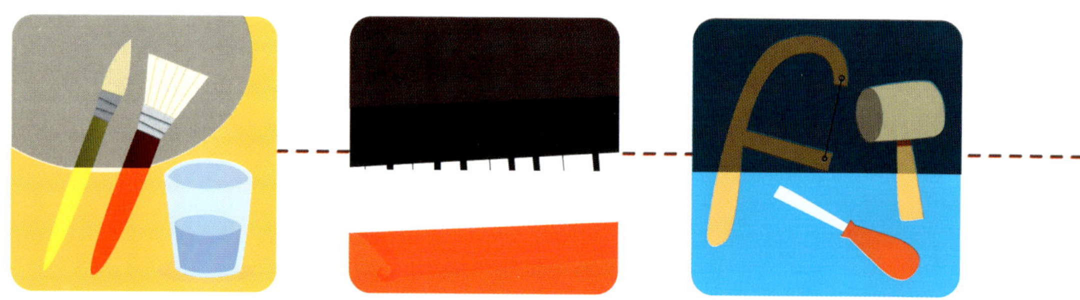

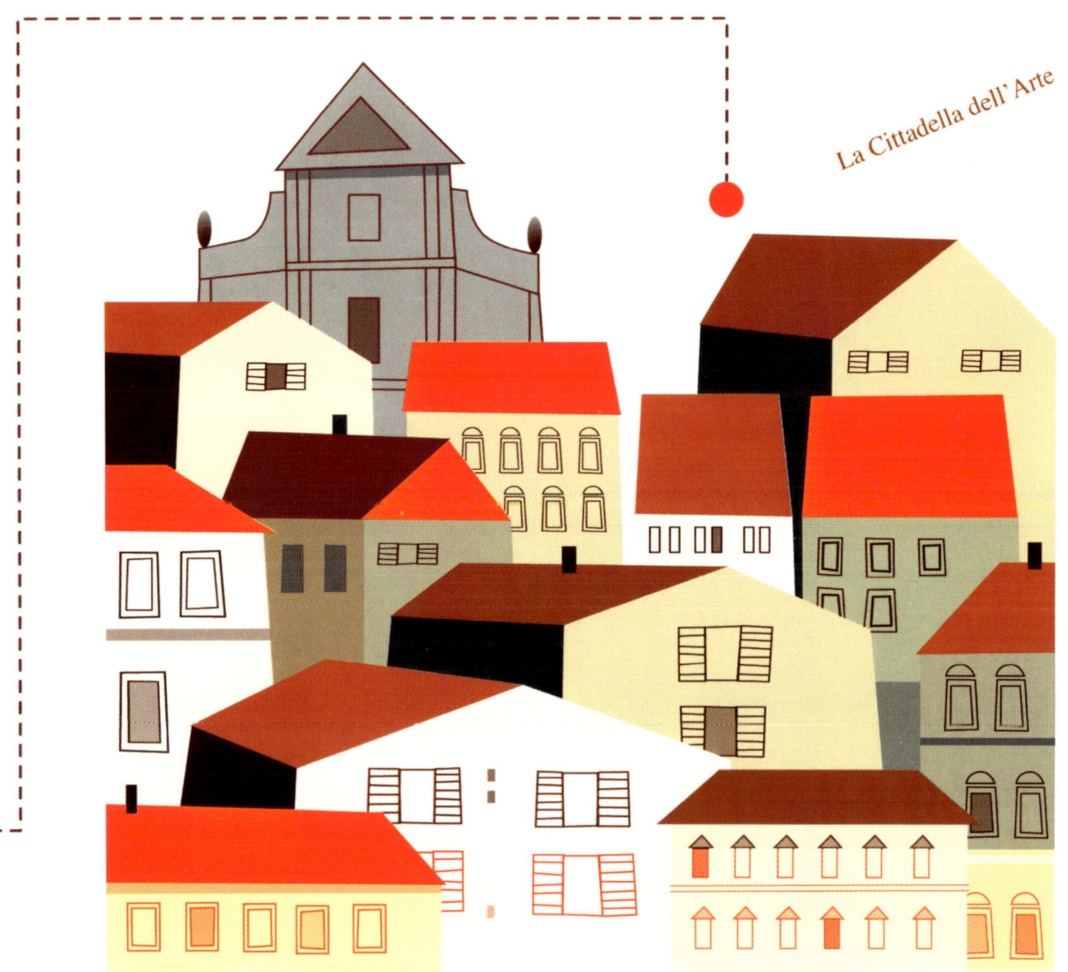
La Cittadella dell' Arte

The Academy was housed in the old hospital of San Matteo. In order to enable future artists to learn by studying the great works of the past, a collection was begun of many age-old works, thereby giving rise to the current museum's core holdings.

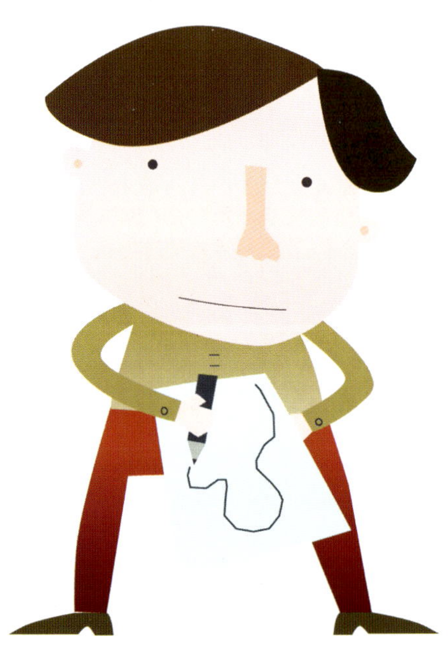

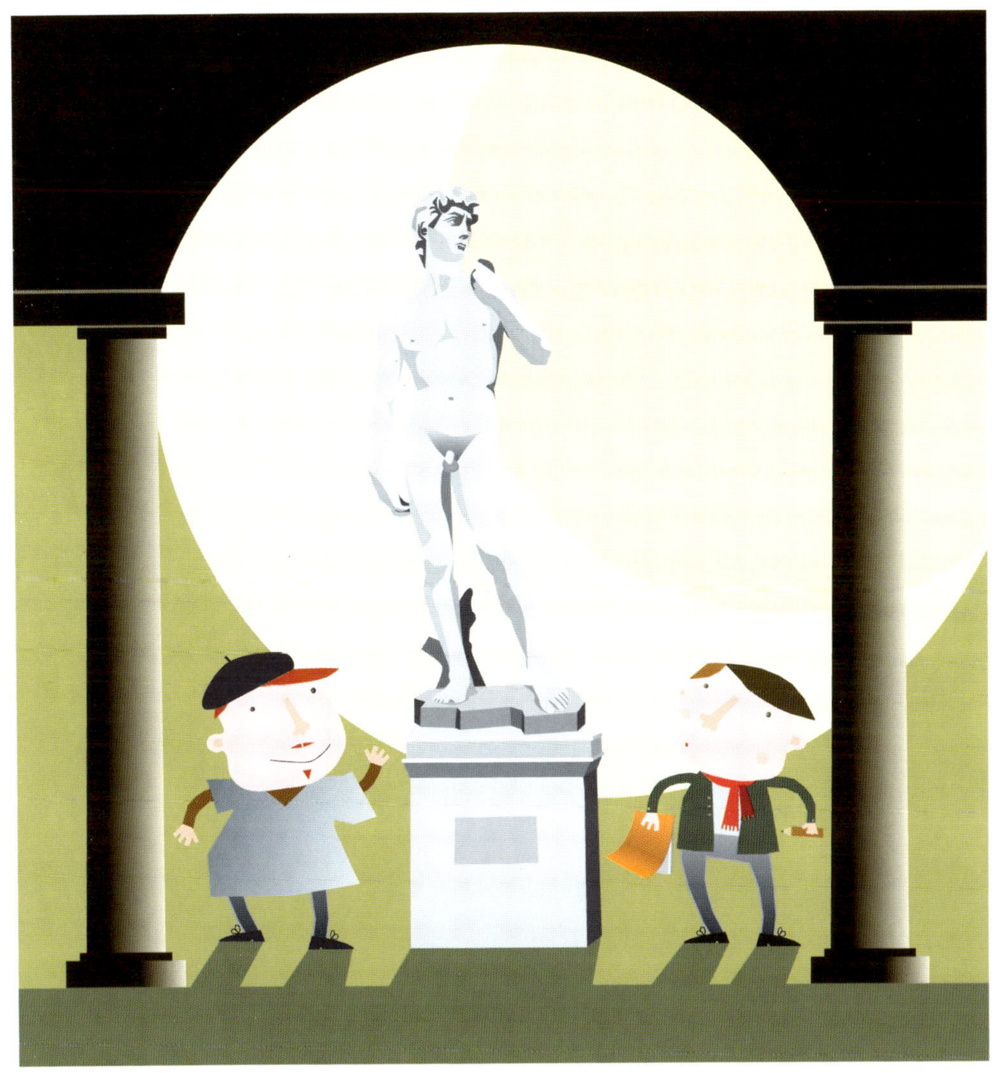

Of course, not all students fancied the idea of having to study and copy past masterpieces. Some, like Giovanni Fattori from Livorno, would simply not hear of spending their days before old statues and paintings. He and his companions instead preferred to while away the day at the nearby *Caffè Michelangiolo*, where he would set the world to rights over coffee. And then someone, making fun of him, said that he was just a *macchiaiolo* (a word referring both the 'splotchy' painting style he adopted and an animal in hiding).

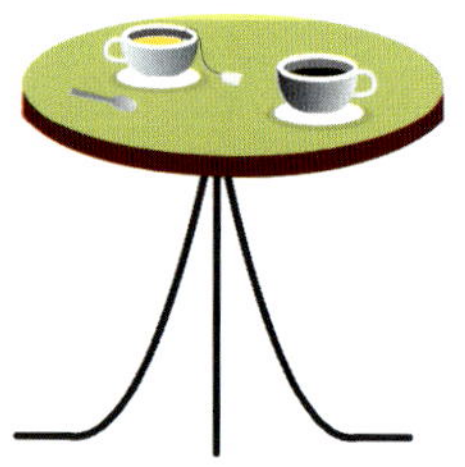
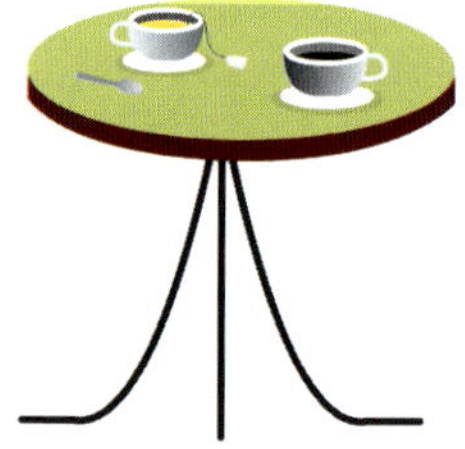
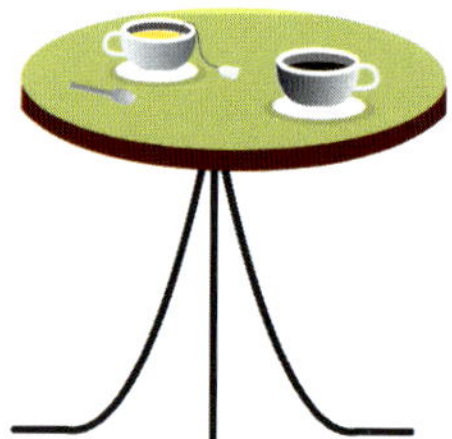

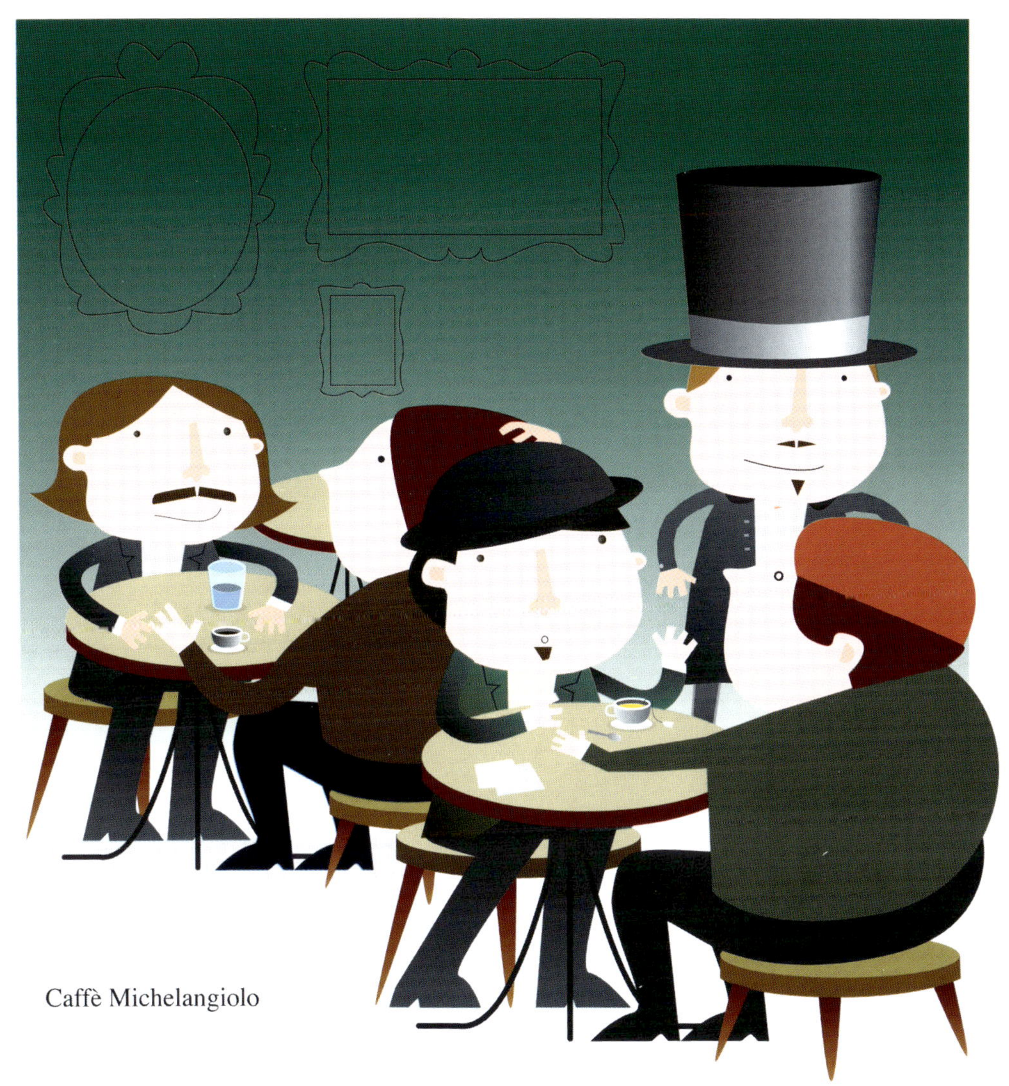

Caffè Michelangiolo

And now for the story of one of the most famous museums in the world, the Accademia. Let's have a look at the map, shall we?

The works on display are divided into to seven groups: Michelangelo's sculptures (*David's Tribune* and the *Prisoners' Gallery*); the *Florentine Rooms*; the *Hall of the Colossus*; the *19th-century Room*; the *Byzantine Rooms*; the *First-Floor Rooms* and the *Musical Instruments Rooms*.

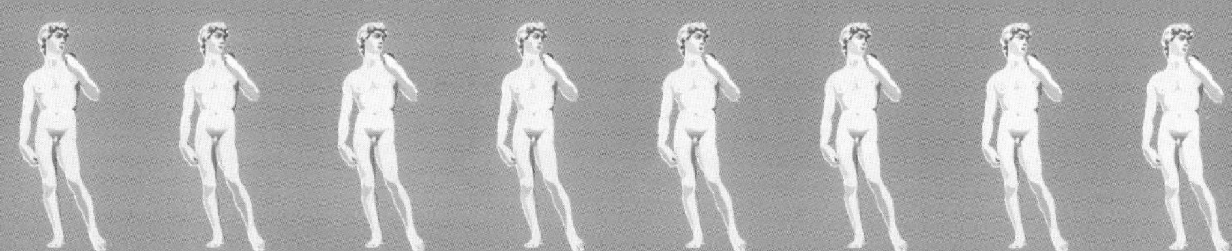

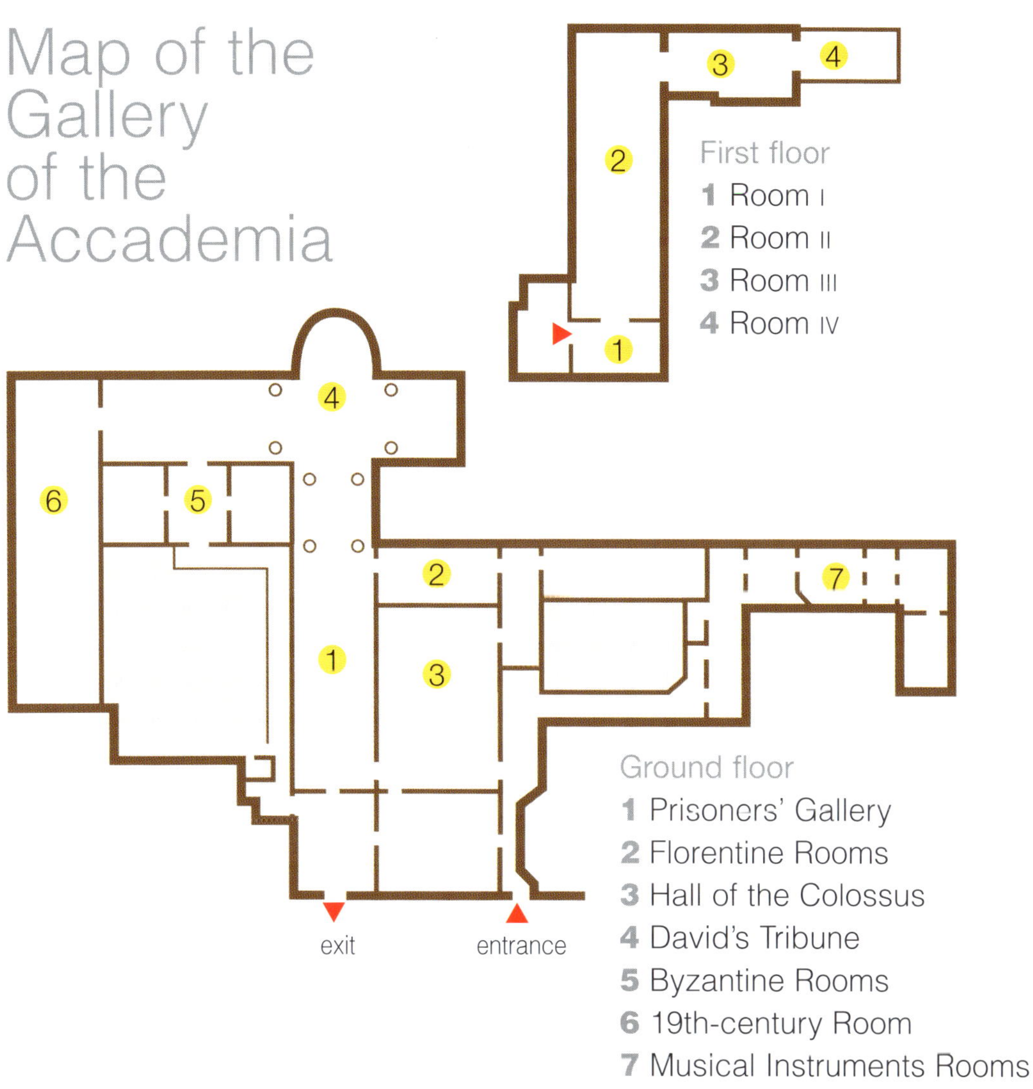
Map of the Gallery of the Accademia
First floor
1 Room I
2 Room II
3 Room III
4 Room IV
Ground floor
1 Prisoners' Gallery
2 Florentine Rooms
3 Hall of the Colossus
4 David's Tribune
5 Byzantine Rooms
6 19th-century Room
7 Musical Instruments Rooms
exit
entrance

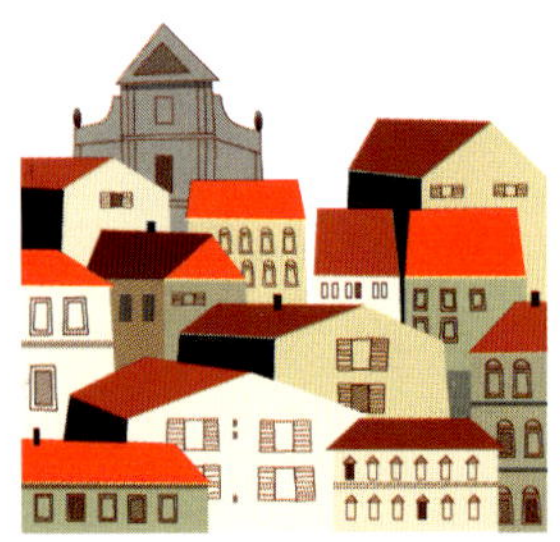

Tribuna del David

David's Tribune

MICHELANGELO BUONARROTI

David, 1501-1504

And there it is, at the back, this museum's acclaimed masterpiece! So that eager visitors could admire the statue in all its majesty, between 1873 and 1882 the Florentine architect Emilio de Fabris (who at the time was also working on the Florence Cathedral façade) built this well-lighted gallery. As even its name, *Tribune*, implies, here, *David* occupies the same revered position as the high altar in a church.

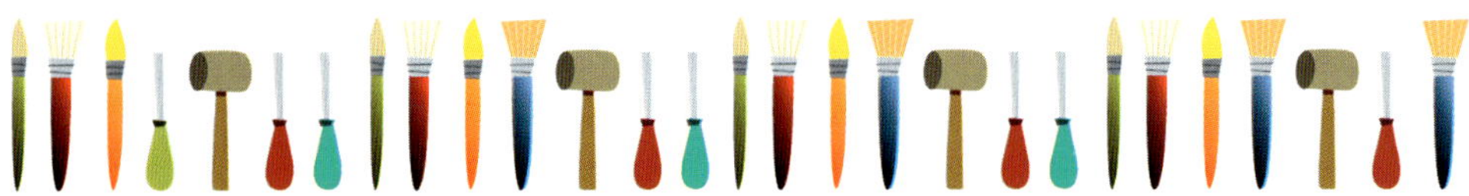

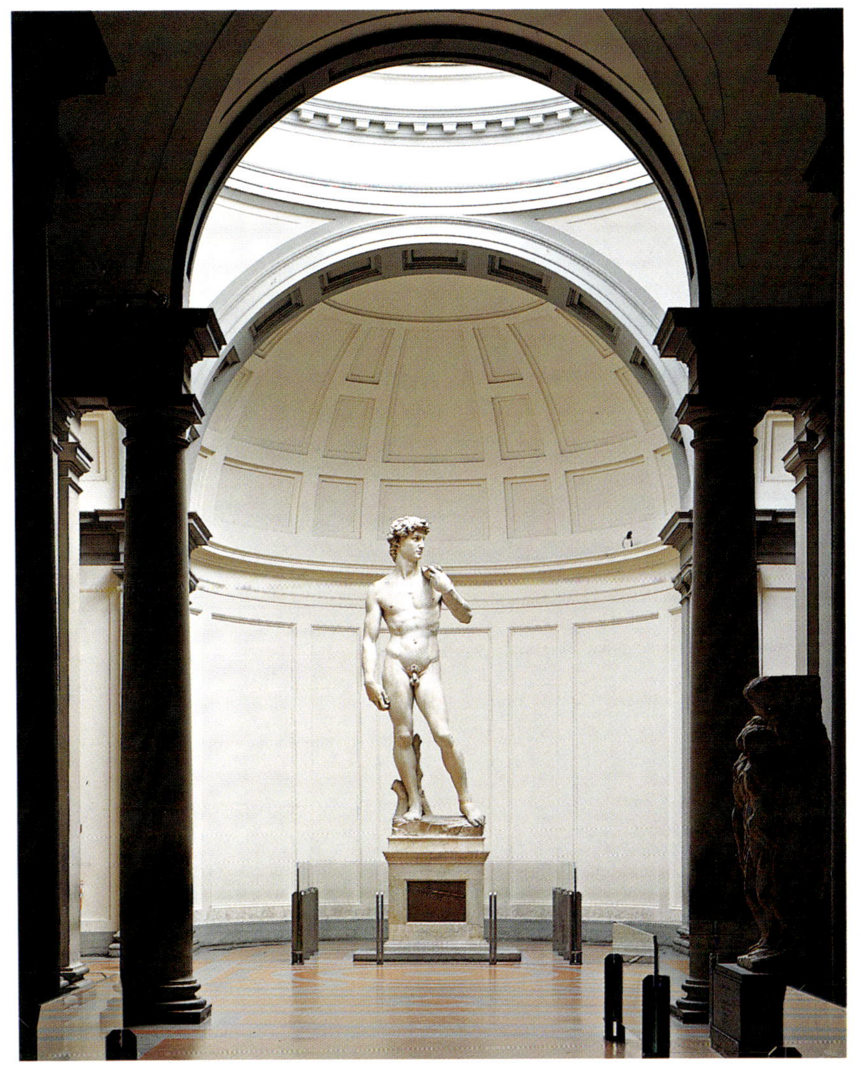

The year was 1501.

The Cathedral workshop of Florence showed the young, but already famous, Michelangelo an extraordinary block of marble, which huge as it was, had nonetheless been left, forgotten in the storehouse. Forty years prior, a sculptor had started to work on it, only to give up in the face of such a monolithic task. Instead, to Michelangelo's strong will and combative nature such a seemingly impossible enterprise represented a challenge that could not be refused, and so he set to work sculpting at once.

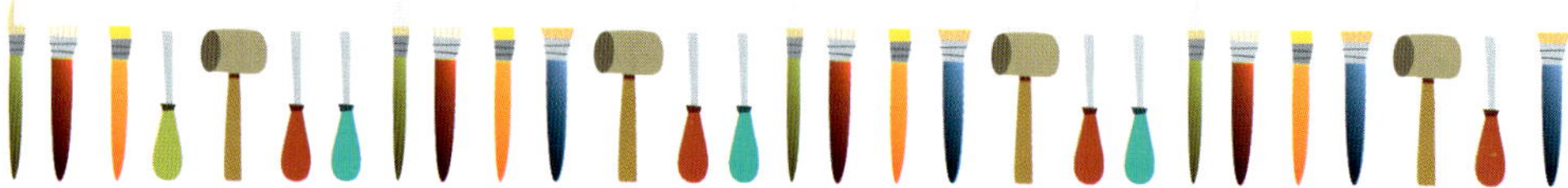

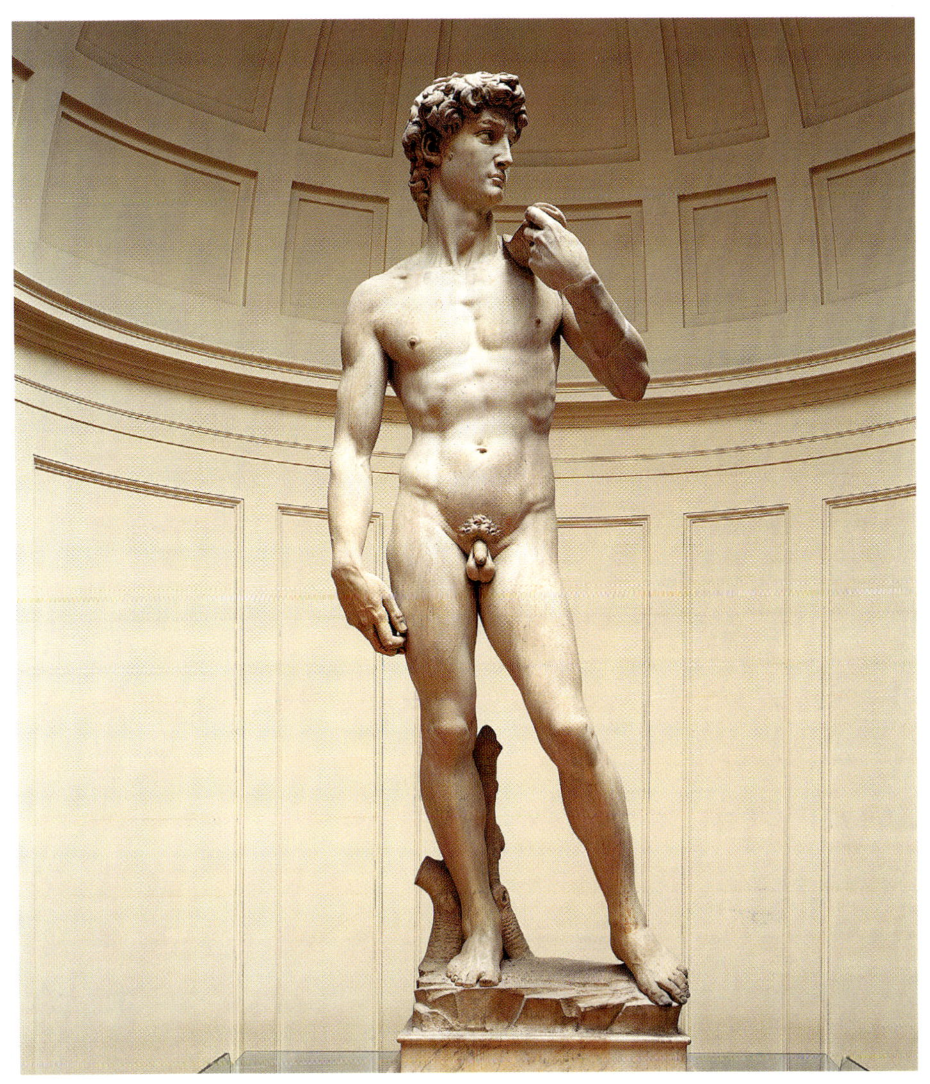

The subject is drawn from the Bible, where David is described as a young shepherd boy who comes to accomplish an extraordinary feat: saving his people from the threat of the giant Goliath. The statue of the biblical hero was supposed to be placed in Florence's cathedral, but when it was finished, those who had commissioned the work were in for a surprise: Michelangelo had sculpted, not a frail young boy, but his inner strength and courage, thus transforming the shepherd boy into the ideal hero of liberty against tyranny.

And worse yet, this David was naked! No, it could not by any means be put in a church!

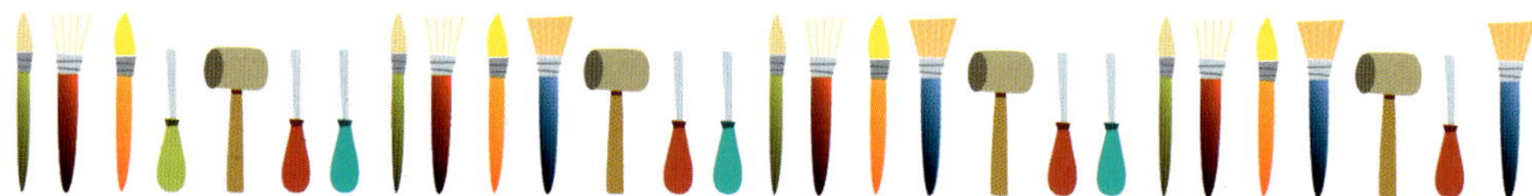

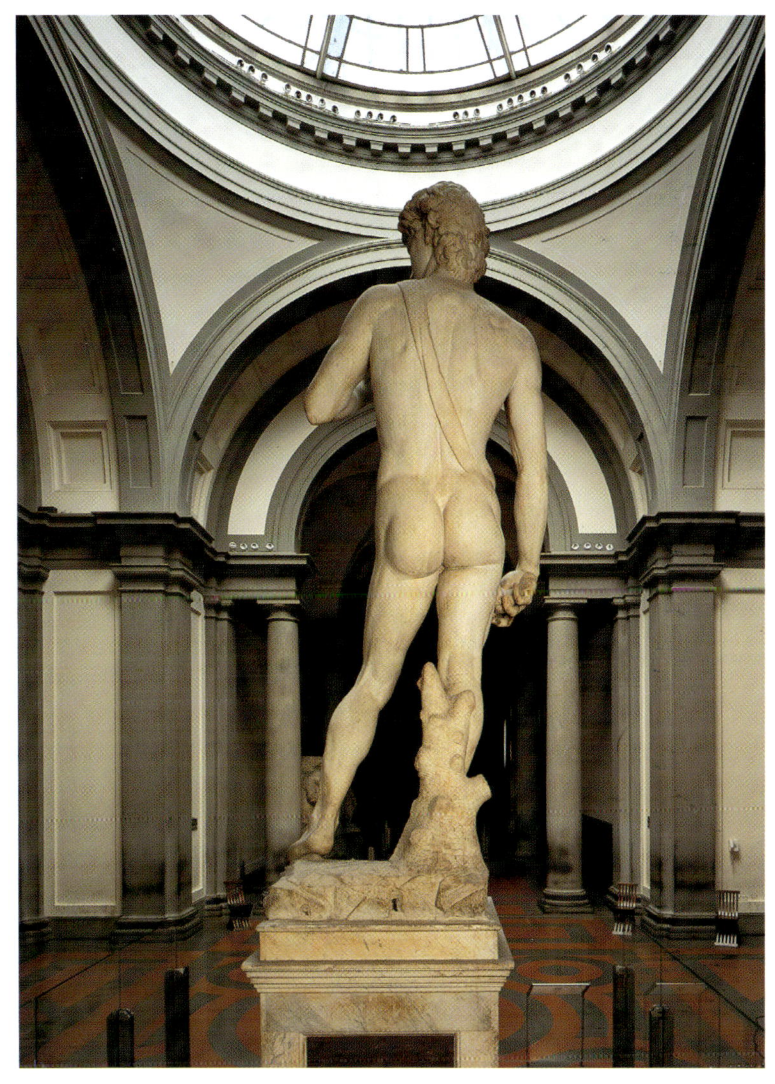

So, a commission of experts was set up to decide the best spot for this giant dilemma. Its members included political leaders, intellectuals and artists, amongst which the great Leonardo da Vinci. Seeing its exceptional quality and the ideals to which it aspired, it was decided that its most natural setting could be none other than the entrance to Palazzo Vecchio, the very centre of Florentine government: there the *Giant* would stand as guardian of civil liberty and pride of the city.

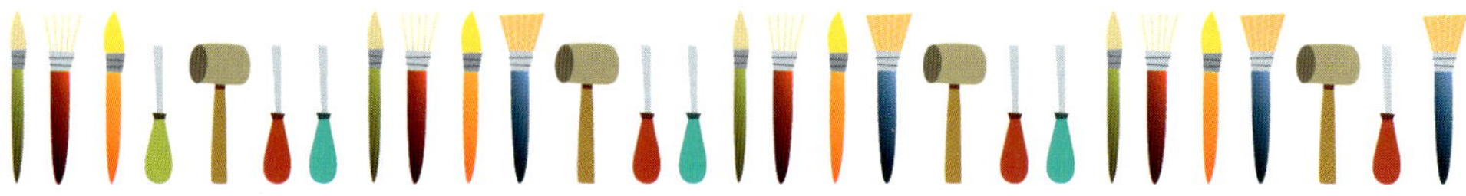

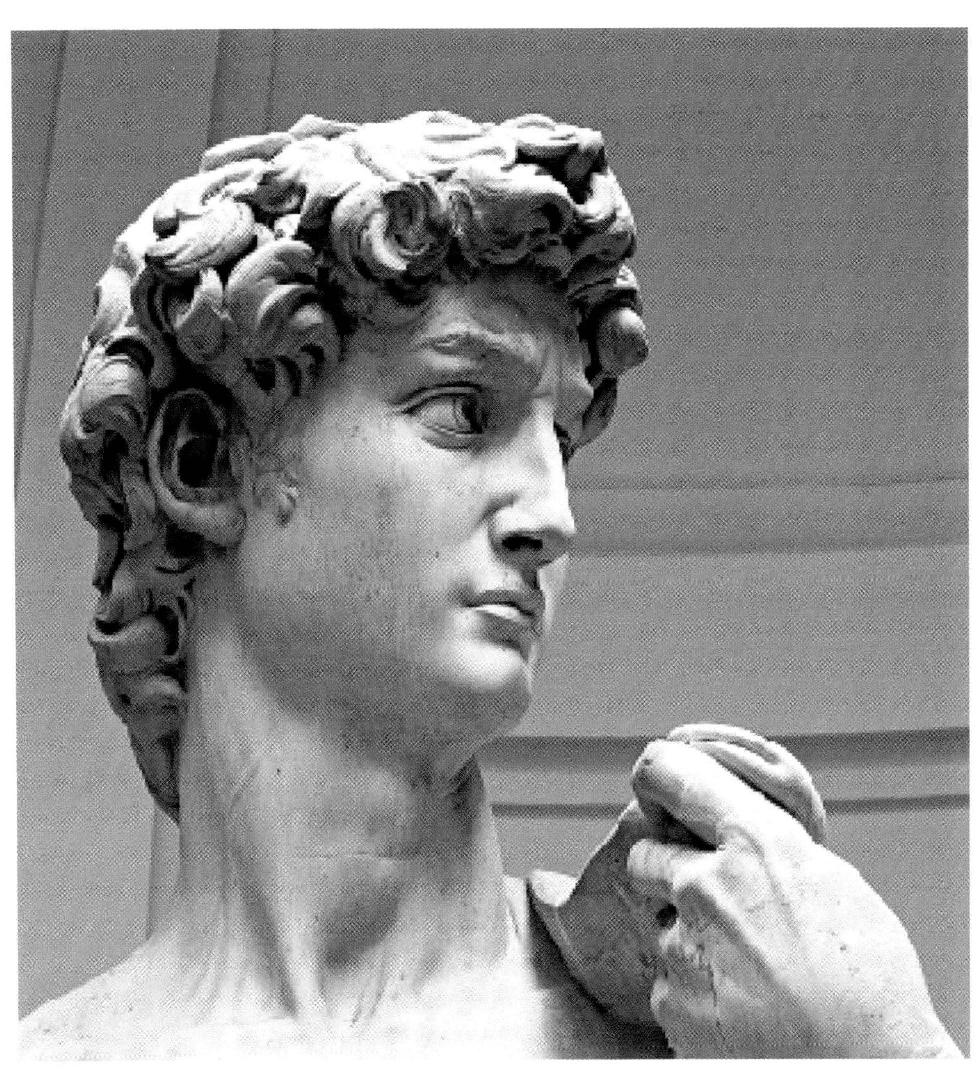

David is portrayed with a sling over his left shoulder, its extremity held firmly in hand by the power of sinewy muscles, which despite the cold lifelessness of the marble, can barely contain the energy coursing through him. And there he was to stand, in Piazza della Signoria, for almost four centuries, becoming one of Florence's most evocative symbols.

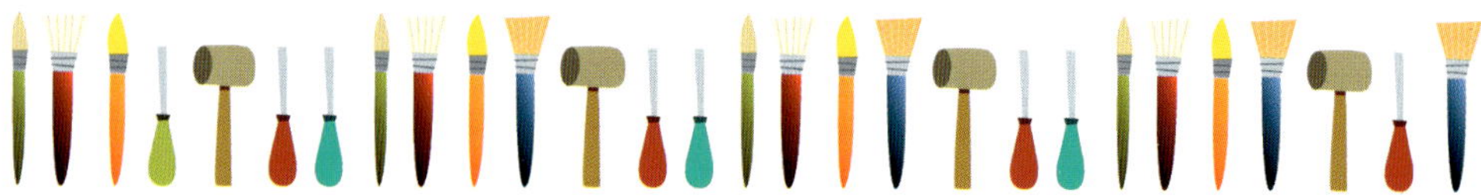

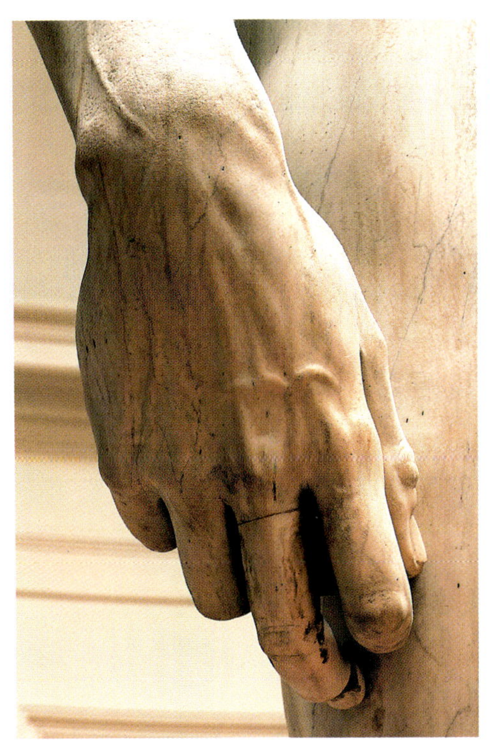

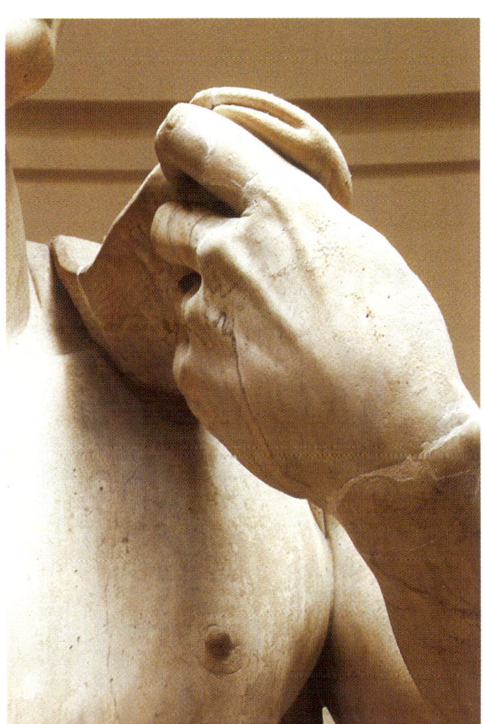

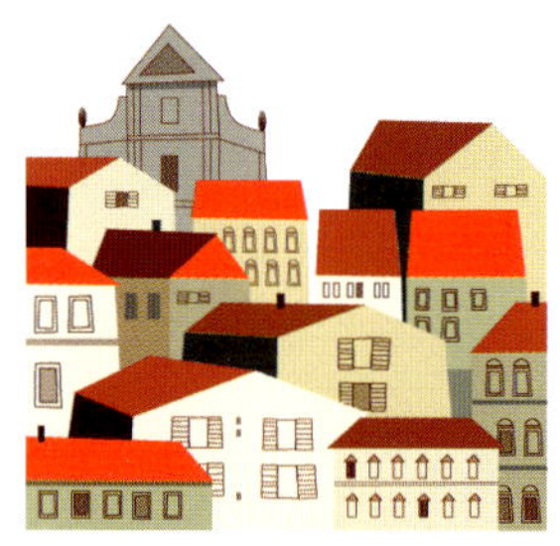

Galleria dei Prigioni

Prisoners' Gallery

Michelangelo Buonarroti and assistants
Palestrina Pietà, ca 1555

During his long artistic career, Michelangelo took up the theme of the Pietà a number of times. A *Pietà* is a depiction of St. Mary holding the dead body of her son for all believers to see and to mourn. This one in the Accademia is one of his last, and was certainly carried out with the help of assistants. Christ's body is completely limp, the head and legs collapsed to one side. The monumental figure of his mother, St. Mary, is barely able to sustain him, while that of Mary Magdalene is so fragile-looking as to be incongruous beside the rest of the composition.

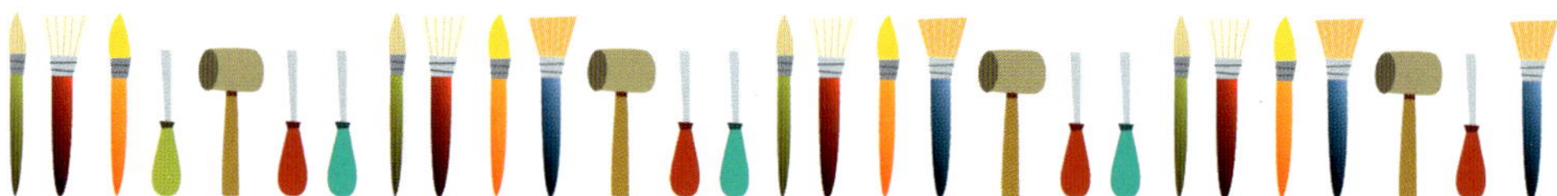

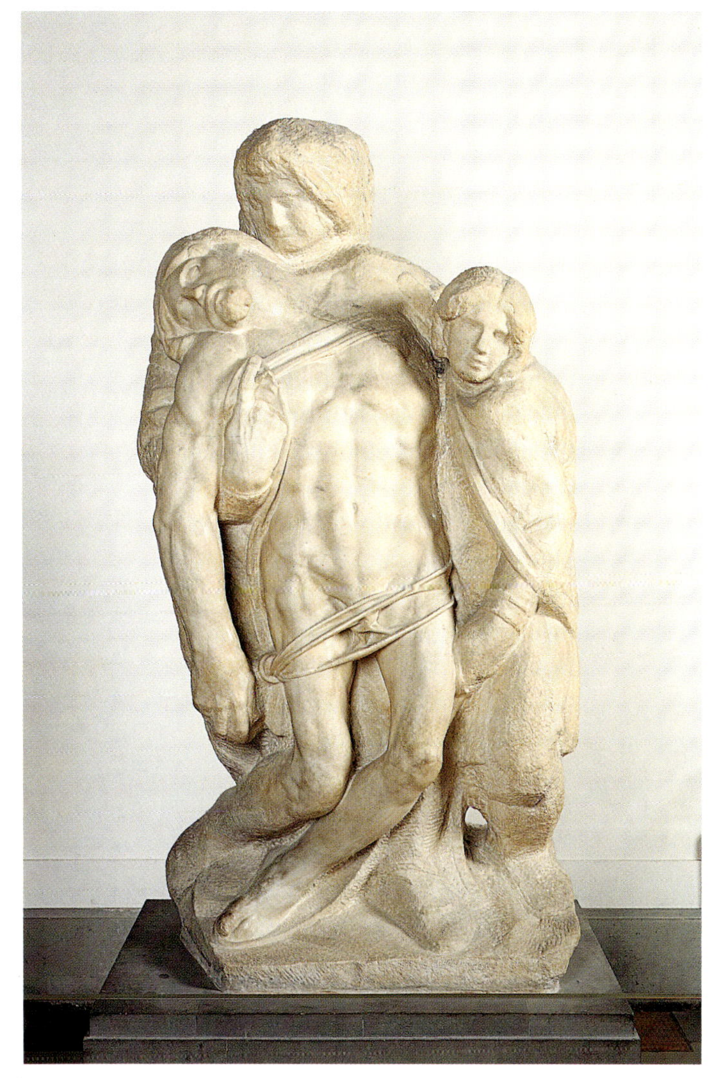

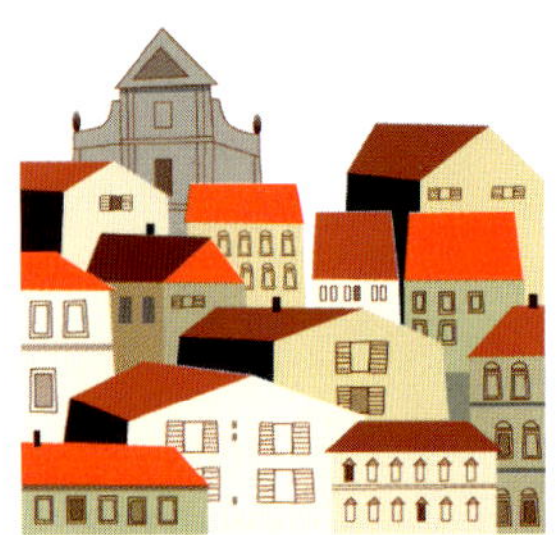

Galleria dei Prigioni

Prisoners' Gallery

MICHELANGELO
The Prisoners, ca 1530

This work, together with its three other unfinished companions, make up the group known as the Prisoners, *or* Slaves. *All originally from Rome, they were meant to adorn a monument in the interior of the Vatican Basilica of St. Peter's. After Michelangelo's death they were donated to the lords of Florence.*

Atlas

The Greek Titan, Atlas, held the world on his shoulders. Michelangelo's instead has his head stuck in a block of marble so heavy that even he cannot raise it to free himself.

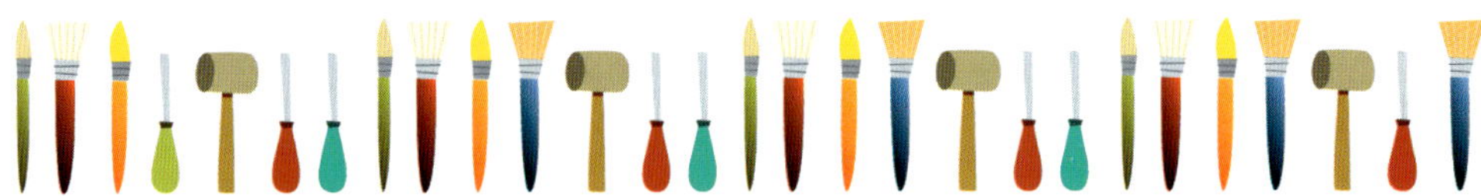

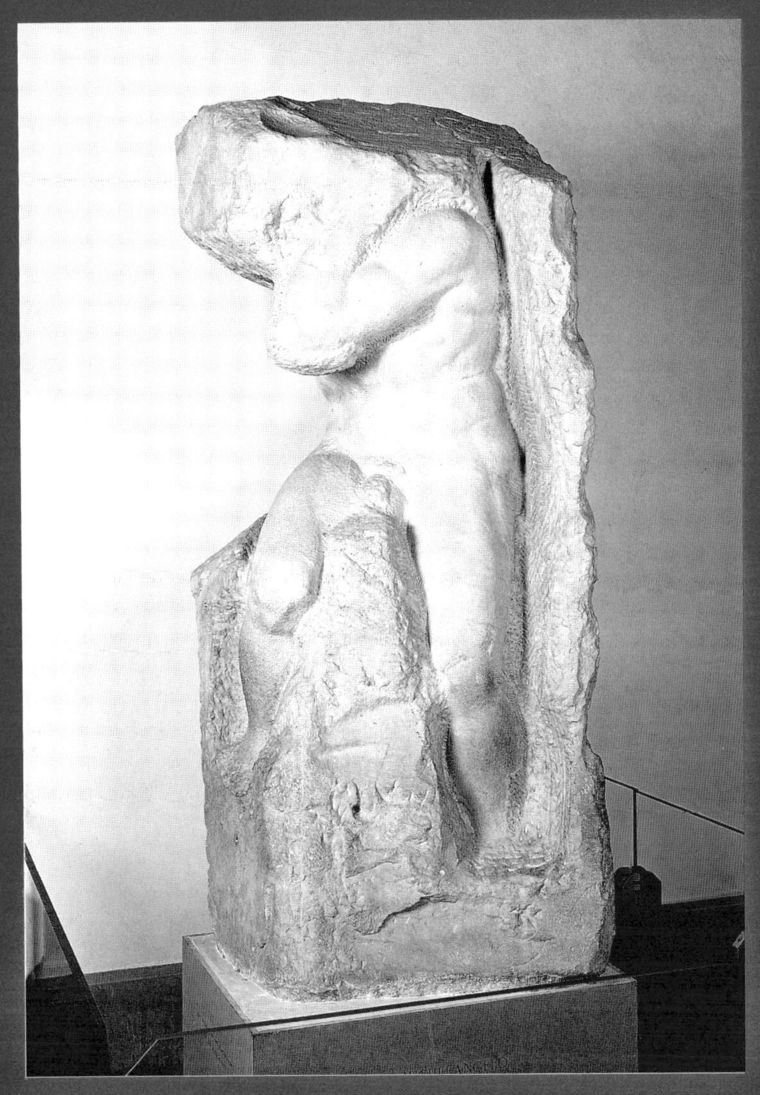

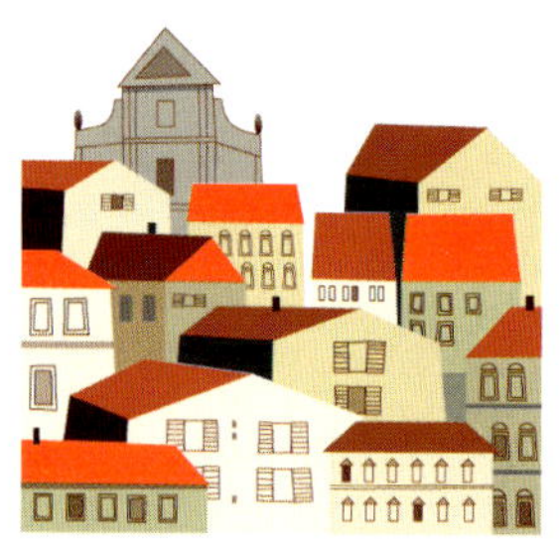

Galleria dei Prigioni

Prisoners' Gallery

MICHELANGELO
The Prisoners, ca 1530

Bearded slave

Such a heavy beard! dishevelled, aggressive... Michelangelo's chisel must have given up against such a force of nature. In fact, he left the work unfinished just at a point where we can nevertheless appreciate the features and, especially, the personality of this hulk: a vigorous, robust figure flawlessly and sensitively fashioned by the great master.

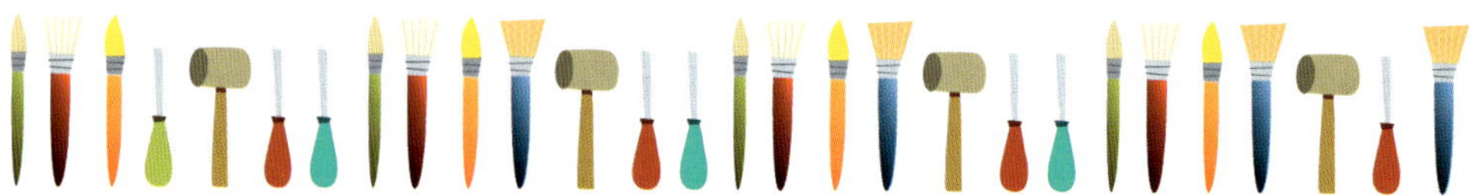

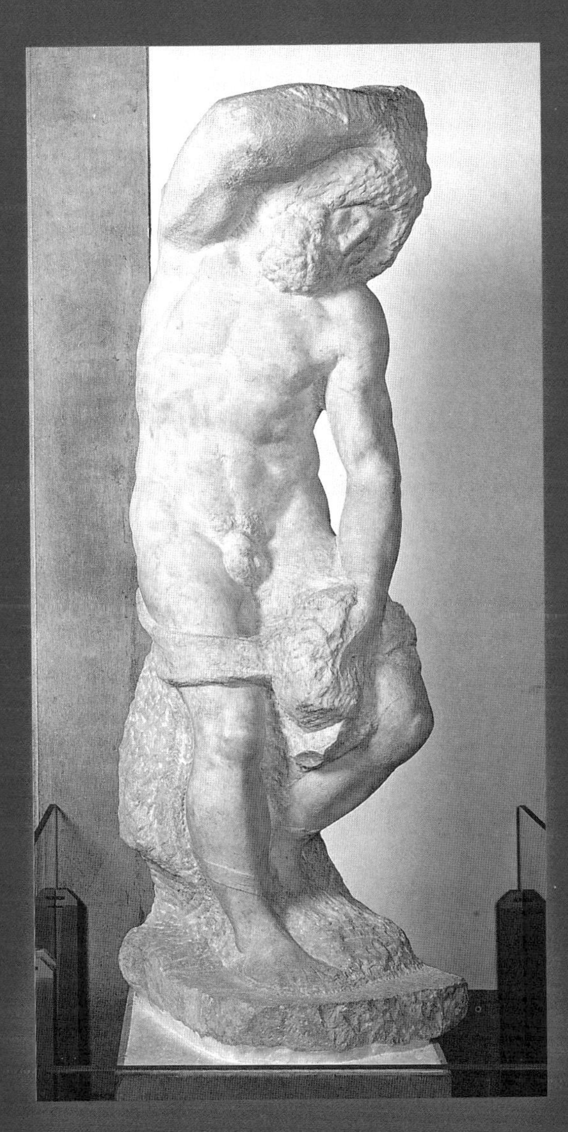

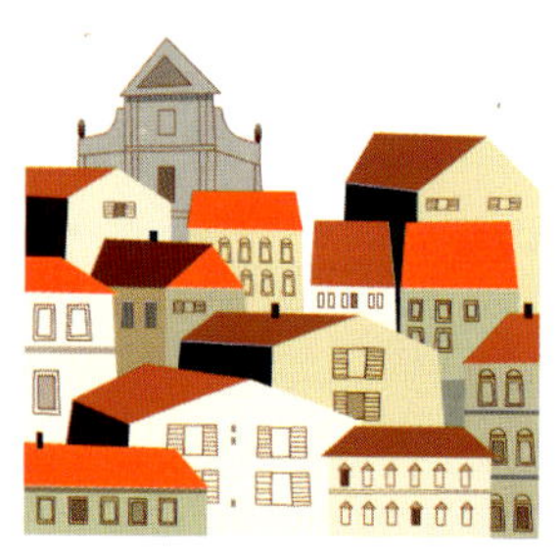

Galleria dei Prigioni

Prisoners' Gallery

MICHELANGELO
St. Matthew, 1506

The apostle Matthew may be old, but he displays the strength of a lion. With an abrupt movement, worthy of a contortionist, he tries to free himself from the burden of the marble holding him back. Although Michelangelo never finished the work, which was destined for the Florence Cathedral, it is so expressive and charged with emotion that it clearly deserves its place here so that it may be seen by all.

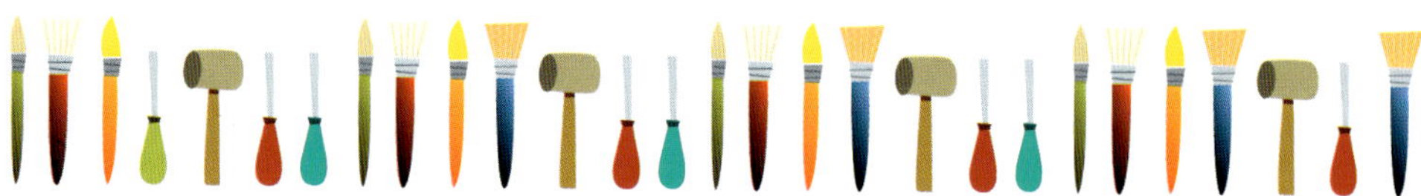

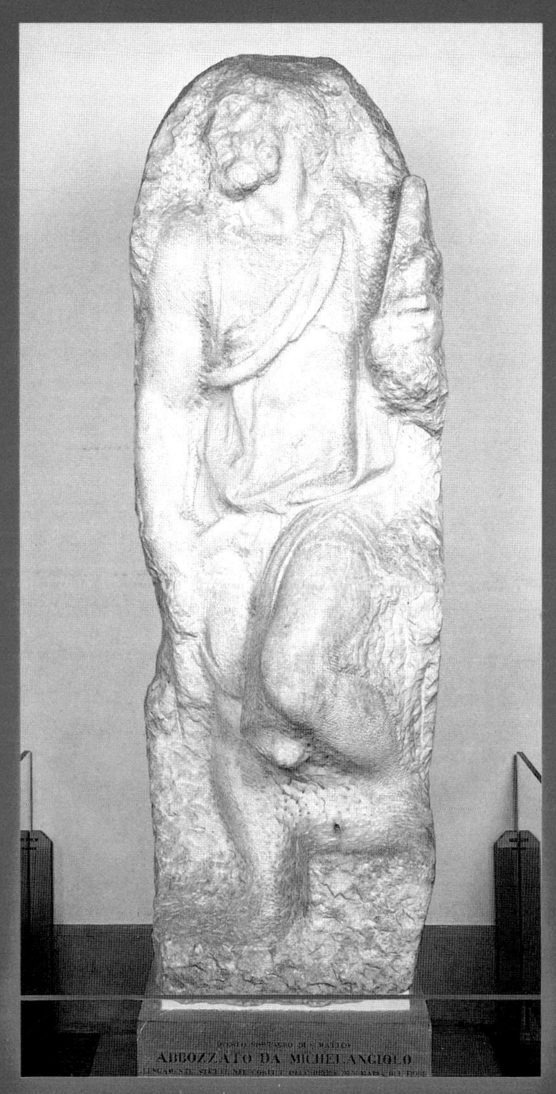
ABBOZZATO DA MICHELANGIOLO

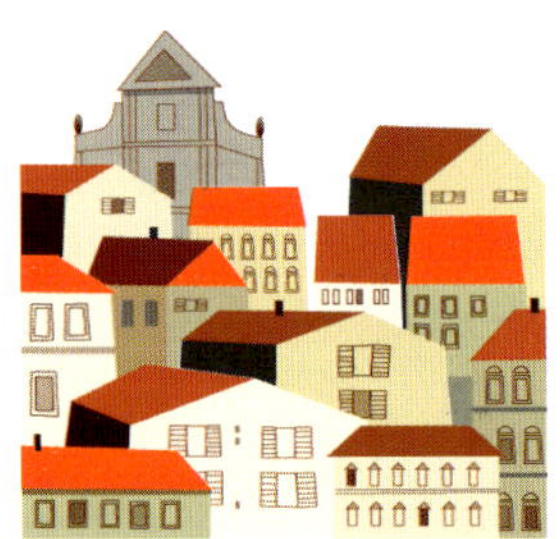

Galleria dei Prigioni

Prisoners' Gallery

MICHELANGELO

The Prisoners, ca 1530

Young slave

What is it that enslaves this man? What keeps him from showing himself, from moving, standing straight up on his own two legs, strong and muscular as they are? The marble block, of course…

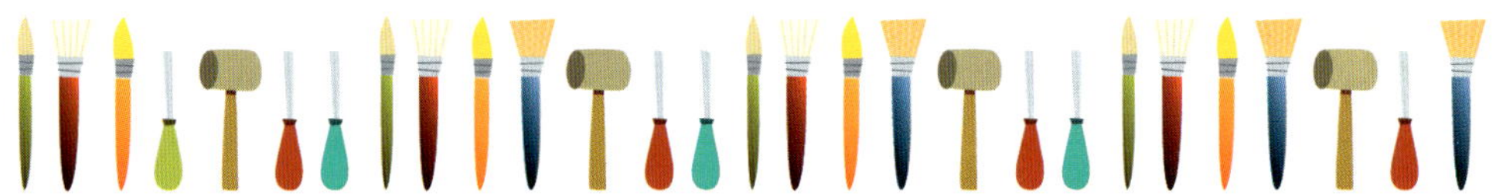

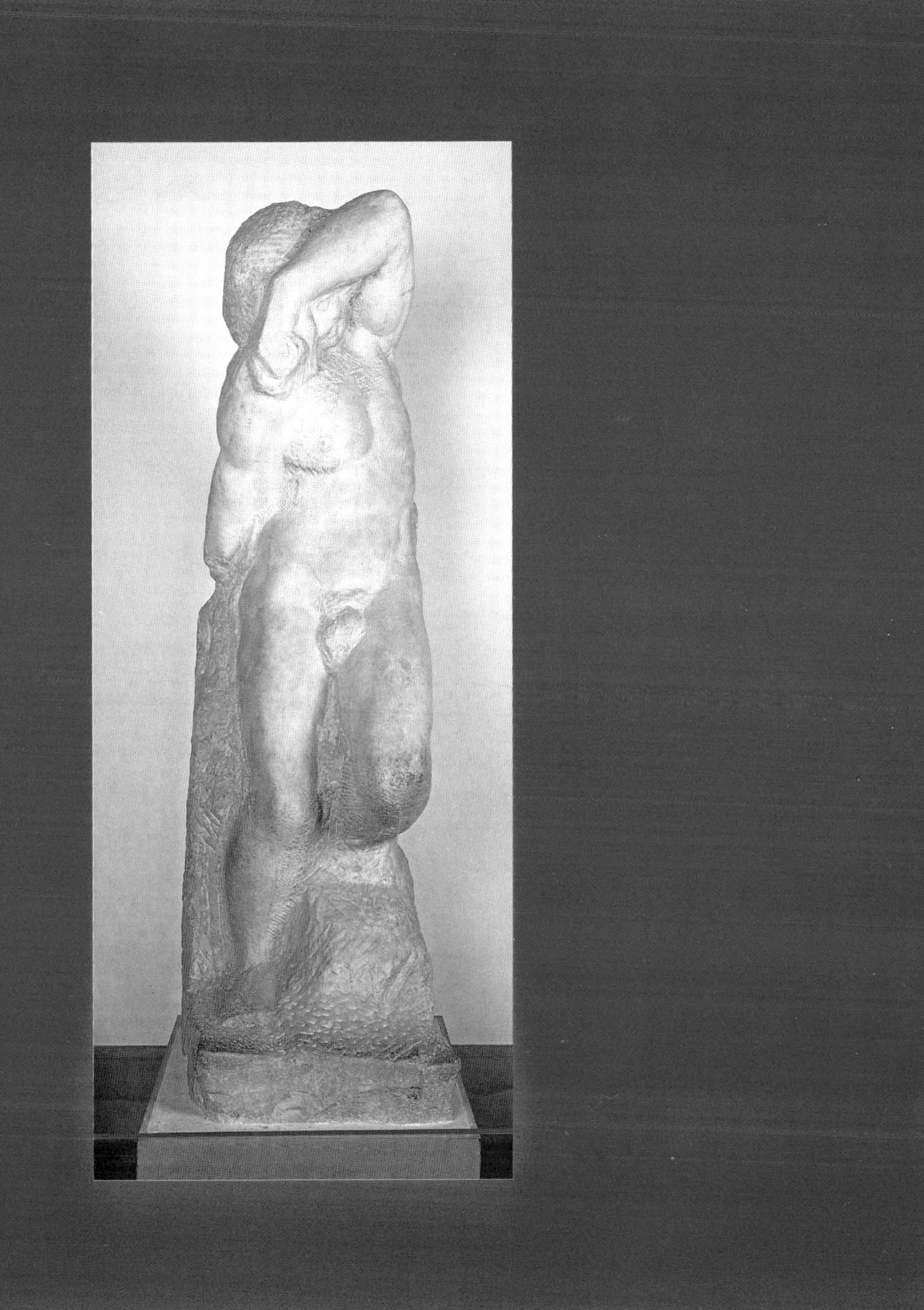

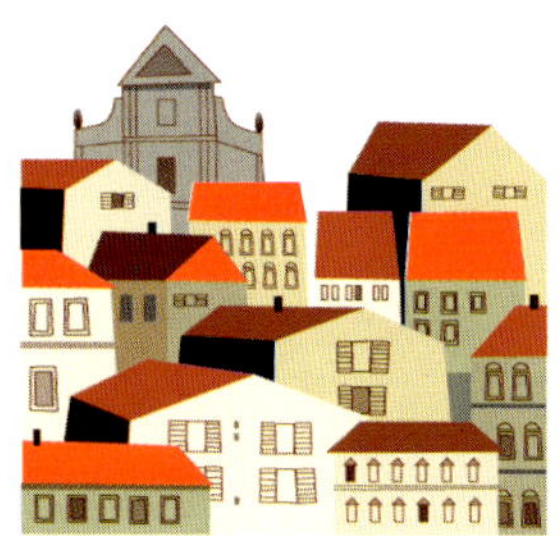

Galleria dei Prigioni

Prisoners' Gallery

MICHELANGELO

The Prisoners, ca 1530

Awakening Slave

An yet, it was not so bad inside that boulder... hidden from sight, a blind eye turned to the all-to-often bitter, wretched world, torpid within the marble's protective caress, life lay dormant therein. And now all this will change: is the performance about to end, or begin?

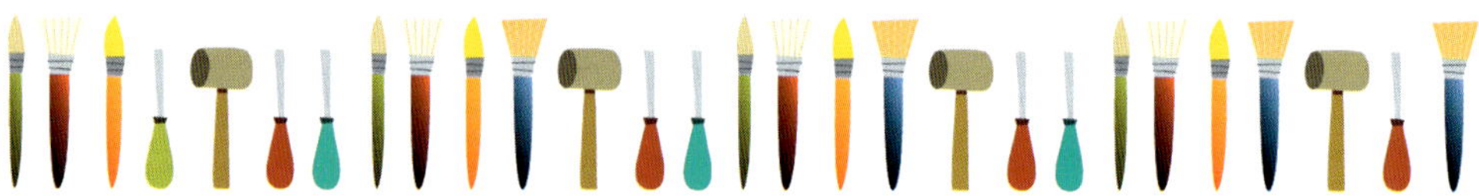

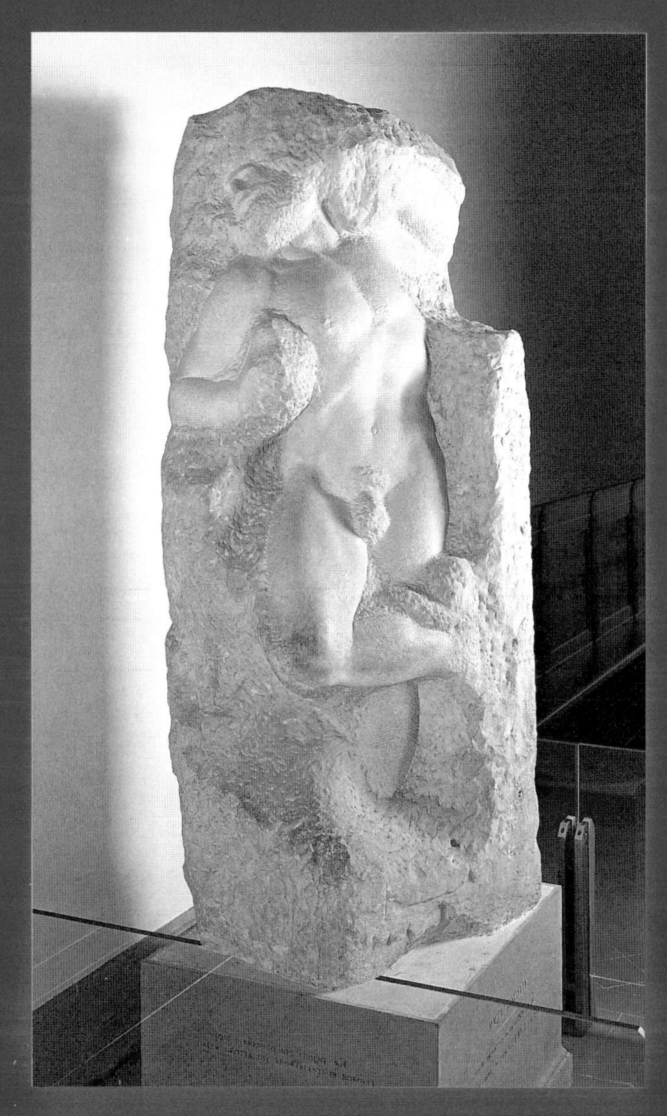

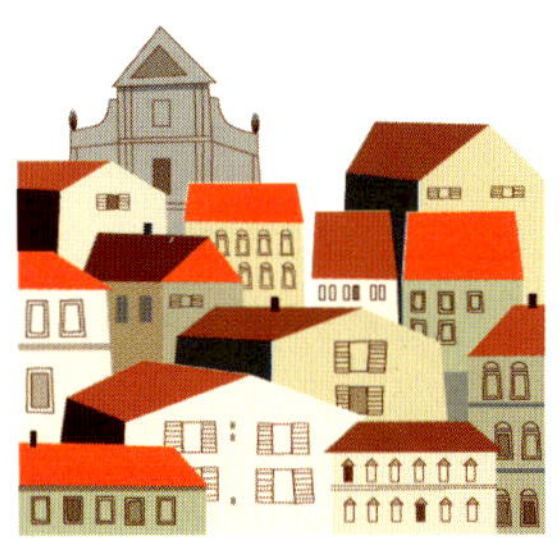

Sale Fiorentine

Florentine Rooms

GIOVANNI DI SER GIOVANNI, KNOWN AS LO SCHEGGIA

Adimari Chest, ca 1450

As the name implies, these rooms hold a collection of Florentine paintings from the 15th century, one of the most fertile periods in the entire history of art.

This large wood plate has long been believed to be the front panel of a bridal chest belonging to the Adimari family, though it may instead have been part of a wall decoration. It depicts a courtly bridal procession winding its festive way through the streets of Florence, passing in front of the Baptistery, accompanied by music, singing and dancing. The men and women in rich flowing robes and brightly coloured hats are depicted down to the very finest detail... But who is the lucky couple?

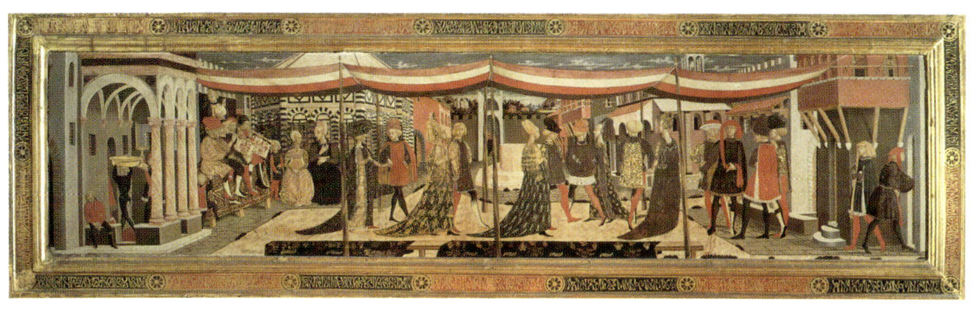

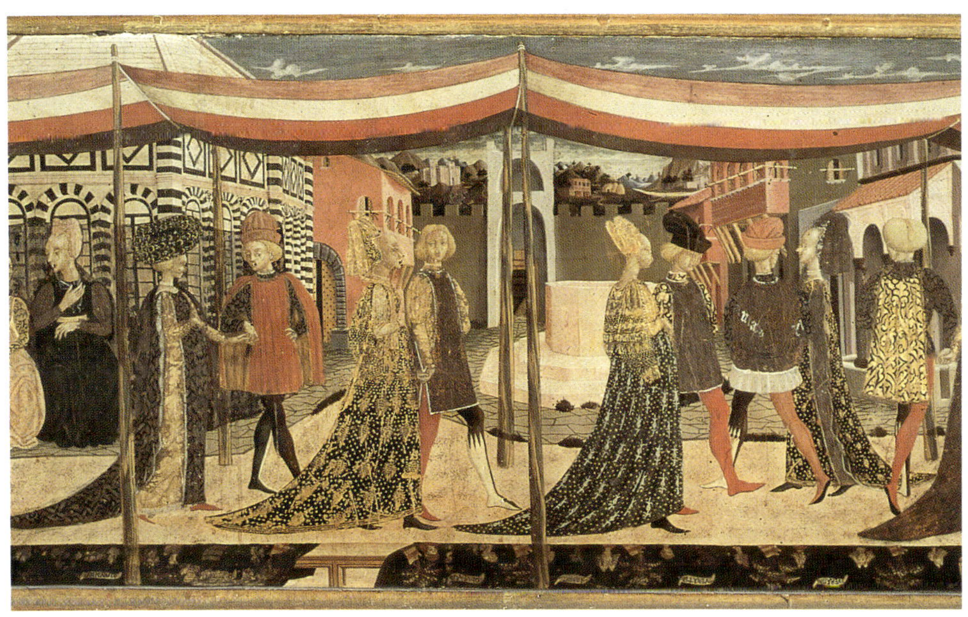

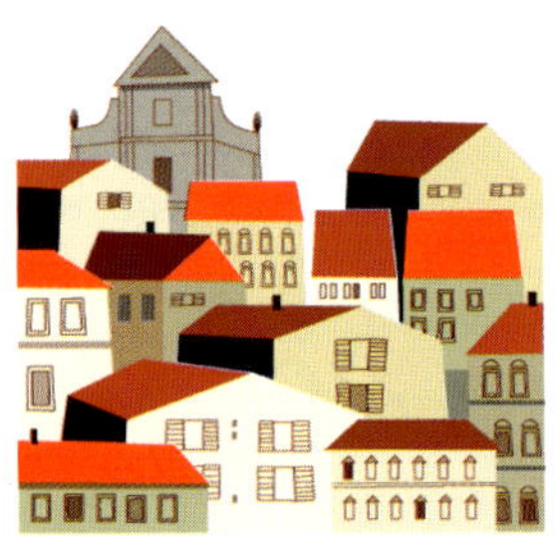

Sale Fiorentine

Florentine Rooms

SANDRO BOTTICELLI, *Madonna and Child with young St. John and two angels*, ca 1468

Botticelli was just over twenty years old when he painted this, and he was already preparing himself to become the graceful, elegant master of the court of Lorenzo the Magnificent. St. Mary, wrapped in a blue, gold-fringed mantle, is in the centre. The other figures are arranged around her in a semicircle: St. John the Baptist, deep in thought with downcast eyes, on the right, and two angels, one of which is helping the young mother to hold the Child Jesus.

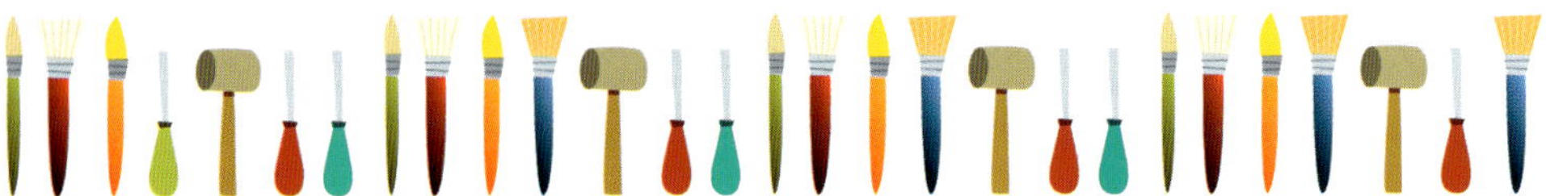

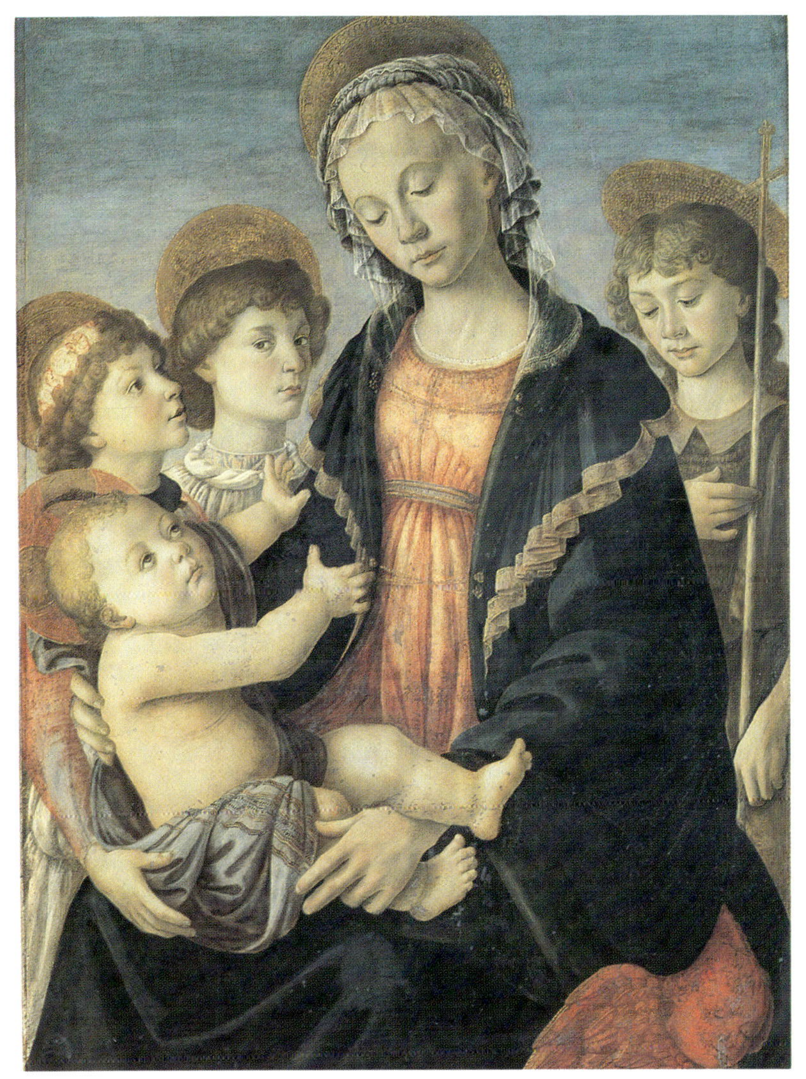

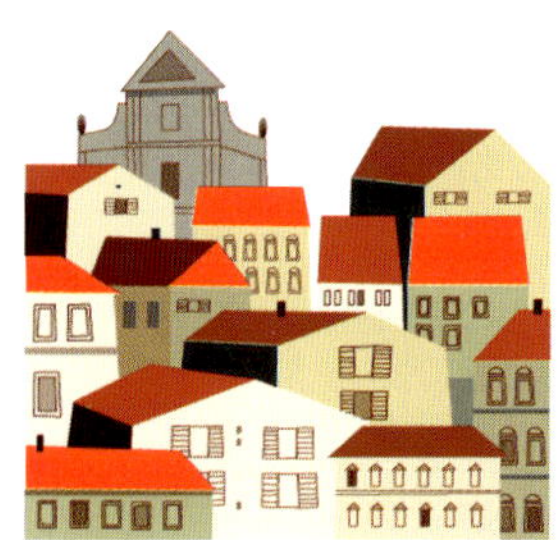

Sala del Colosso

Hall of the Colossus

GIAMBOLOGNA

Rape of the Sabine Women, plaster cast, 1582

This room's name dates back to the 19th century, when it was used to hold an enormous plaster sculpture, though the name continuous to be appropriate today…

This is the plaster model used by the Flemish sculptor, Jean de Boulogne (known as Giambologna in Florence), to sculpt the marble statue now in Piazza della Signoria. Like Michelangelo, Giambologna also wished to test his mettle with oversized statues! The inspiration for the work comes from ancient Roman history and the Gaul's attempt to abduct the women of Rome. The invaders have forcibly taken hold of a woman: the three figures are so tightly knit and communicate such motion that we are prompted to circle the work to view it from all points of view.

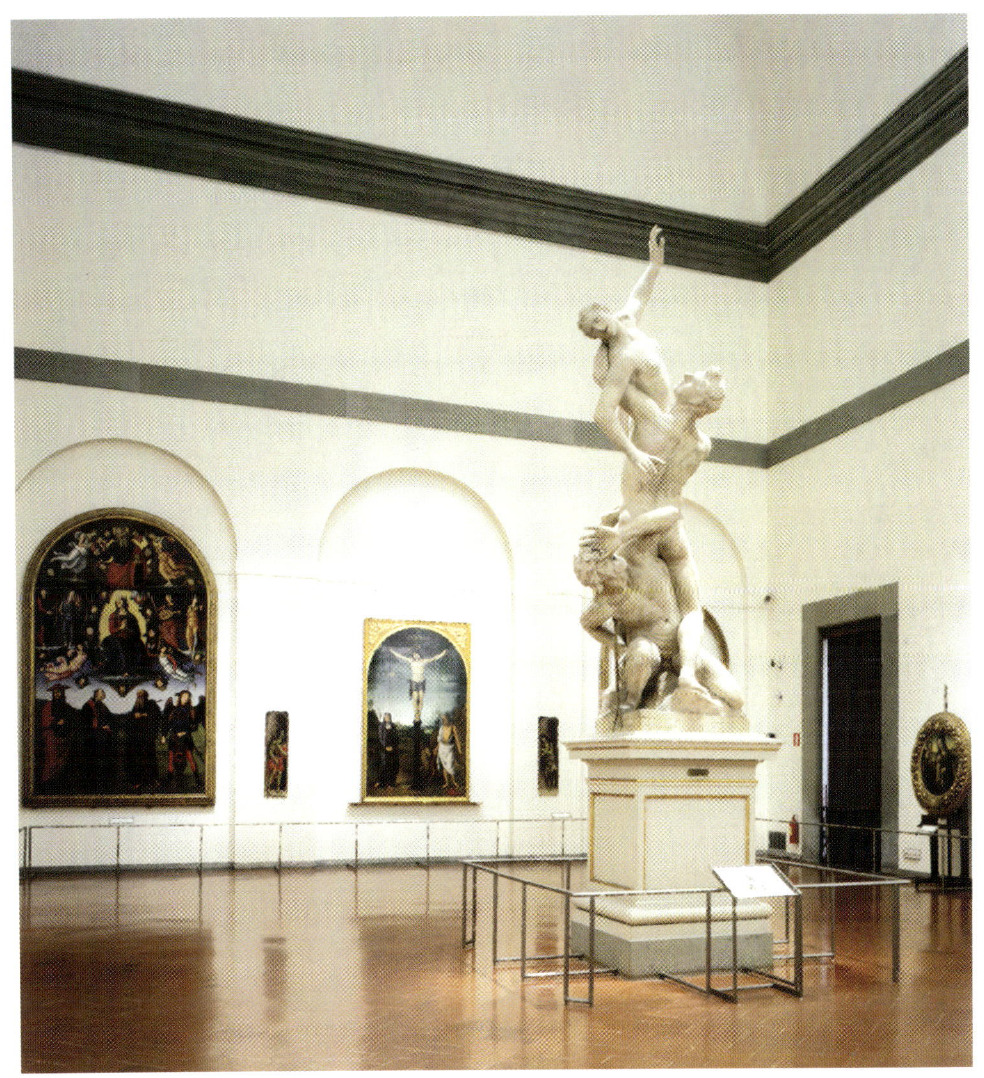

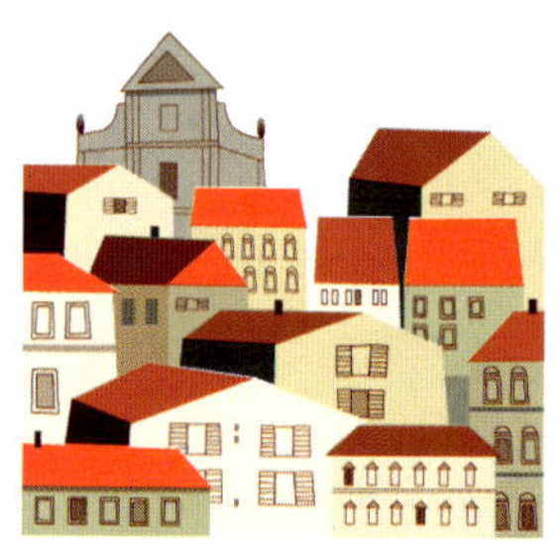

Sala del Colosso

Hall of the Colossus

FRA' BARTOLOMEO DELLA PORTA

The Prophet Isaiah, 1514-1515

Together with the *Prophet Job* and an even larger painting of *Jesus and the Evangelists* (now at the Palatine Gallery in Palazzo Pitti) this work was part of a group that the painter monk executed for the church of Santissima Annunziata. Isaiah, who foretold the birth of Christ, is dressed in clothes of the time, with an unusual hat and rich mantle which dazzles the eyes in its colours, especially the yellow-orange clashing with the bright pink hues of the robe.

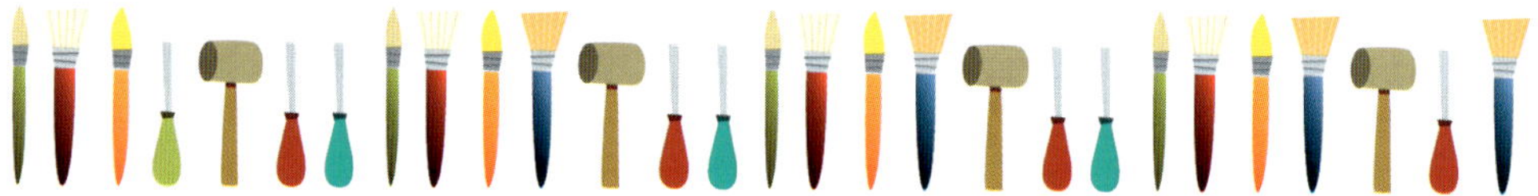

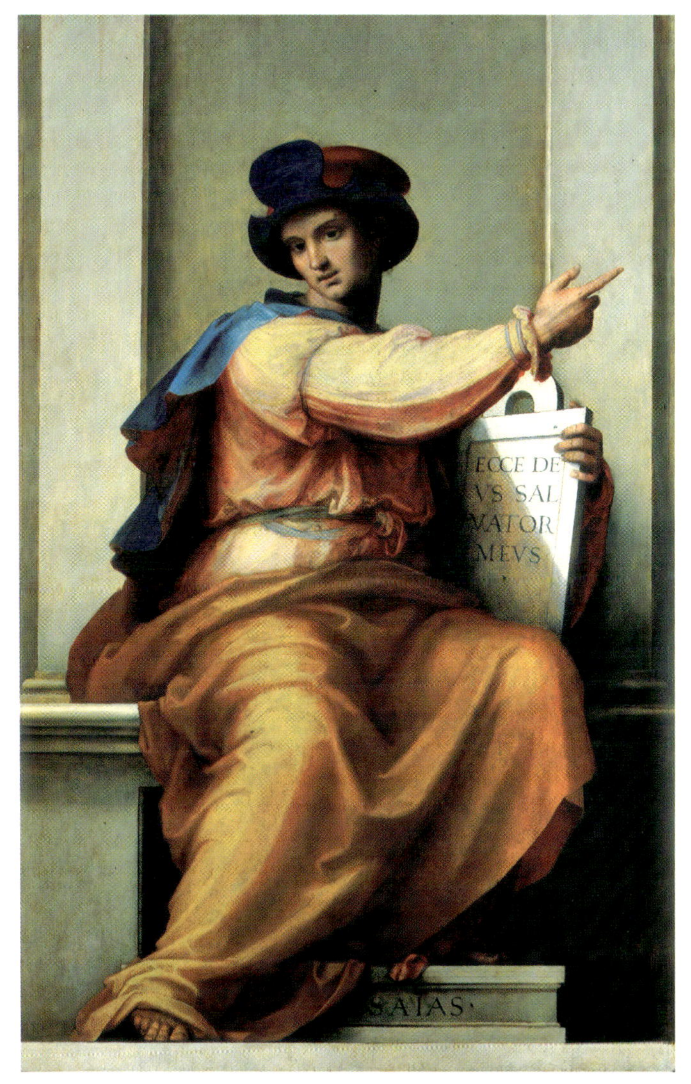
ECCE DE
VS SAL
VATOR
MEVS
SAIAS

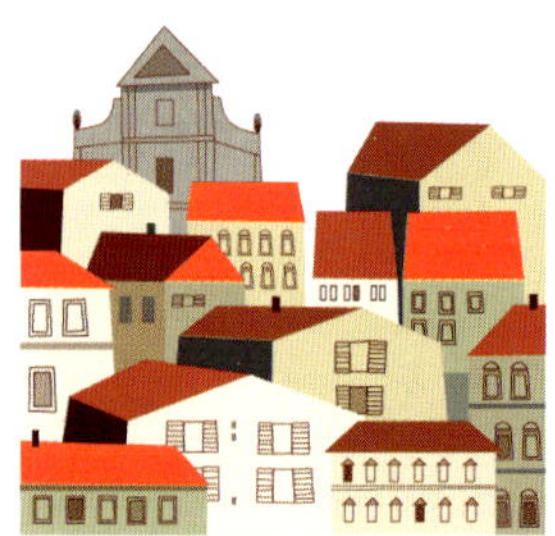

Salone dell'Ottocento

19th-century Room

The Bartolini plaster collection

This large room, which was originally a sick ward in the hospital of San Matteo, now holds an extensive collection of the plaster casts that artists used as models, study pieces or for tests. Their presence in this wide open space can help conjure up visions of the bustling activity that must have taken place here, with teachers and students hard at work within the prestigious Academy of Art.

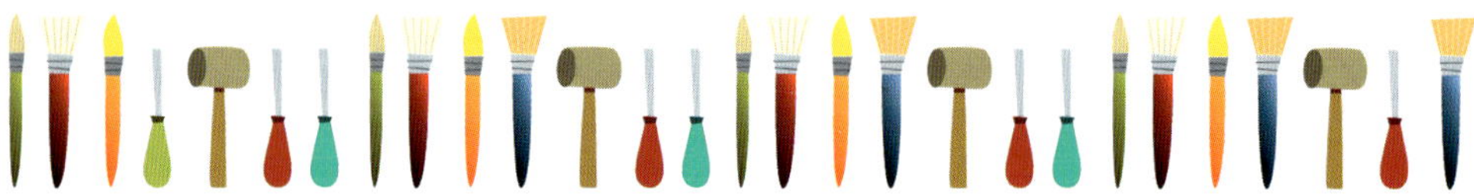

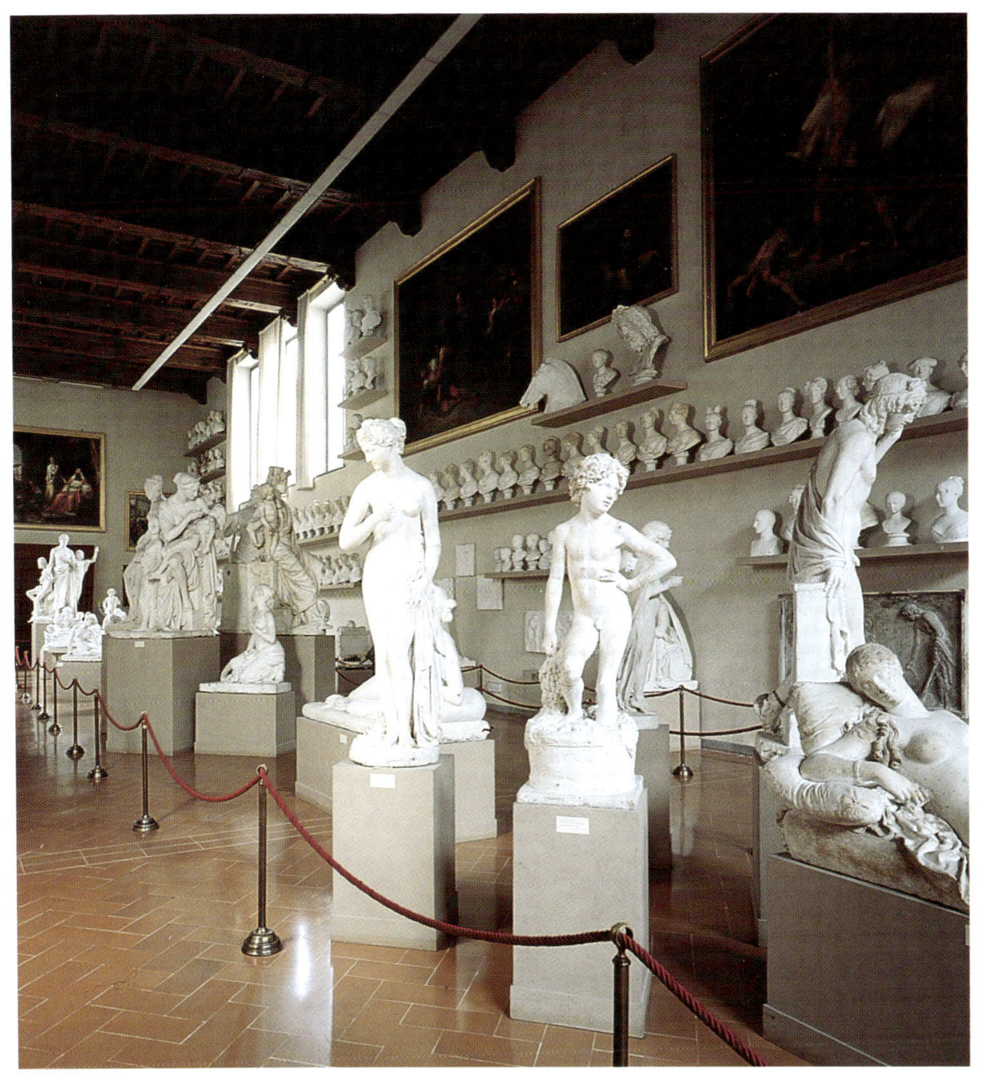

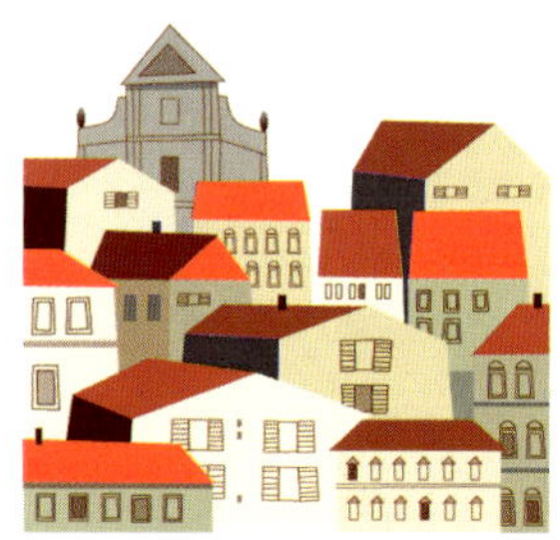

Salone dell'Ottocento

19th-century Room

LORENZO BARTOLINI
Demidoff Monument, post 1828

The Academy's most famous teacher was the sculptor Lorenzo Bartolini (1777-1850). As a young man he had been to Paris and was admired by no less than Napoleon himself. He worked many years in Florence, teaching his students to appreciate both the ideals of classical art and direct observation of life, even if not always beautiful or pleasant.

He was famous for his portraits, religious works and funeral monuments.

Even in the city of Michelangelo, the monument he executed for the rich and powerful Russian Demidoff family represents a true homage to sculpture!

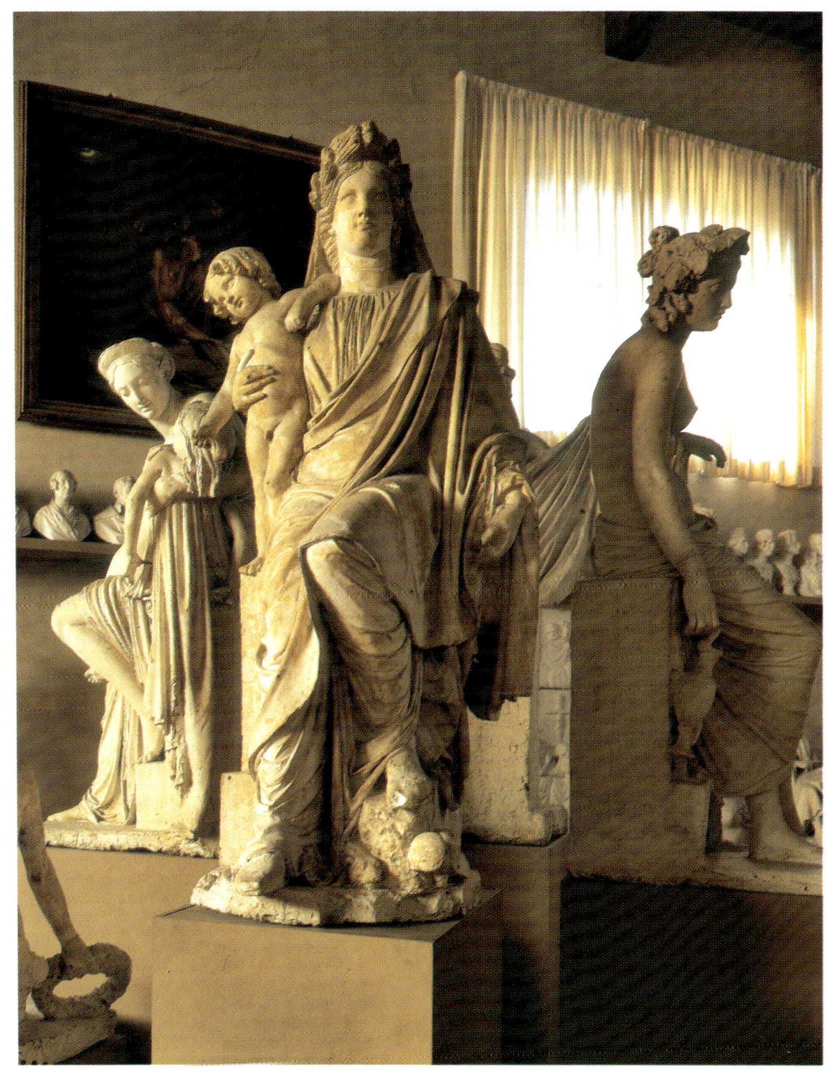

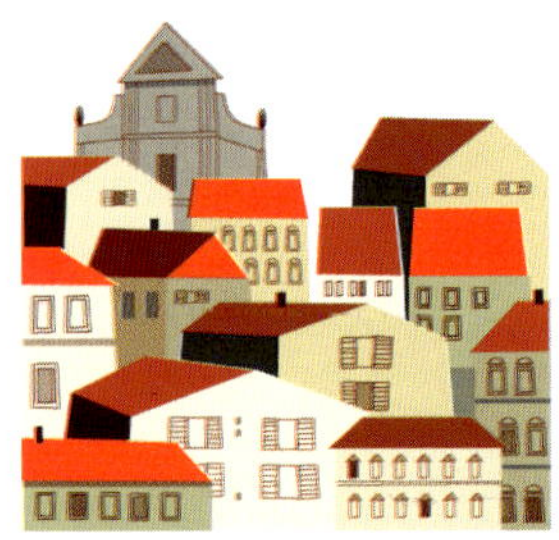

Sale Bizantine

Byzantine Rooms

PACINO DI BUONAGUIDA

Tree of Life, 1305-1310

This is an important section that holds a collection of noteworthy works of medieval Florentine painting. The various religious paintings on wood all bear the rich gold backing of the Byzantine tradition, typical of the period.

This unusual painting, by a contemporary of Giotto, is a rich story told in images: above, an orderly multitude of saints and angels crowds together before Jesus and St. Mary; in the centre is Christ on the Cross, represented in the Franciscan tradition as the Tree of Life, whose branches sprout circles bearing episodes in Christ's life; below the scroll-bearing prophets at the bottom are scenes from *Genesis*, from the *Creation of Mankind* to *Adam and Eve's expulsion from the Garden of Eden*.

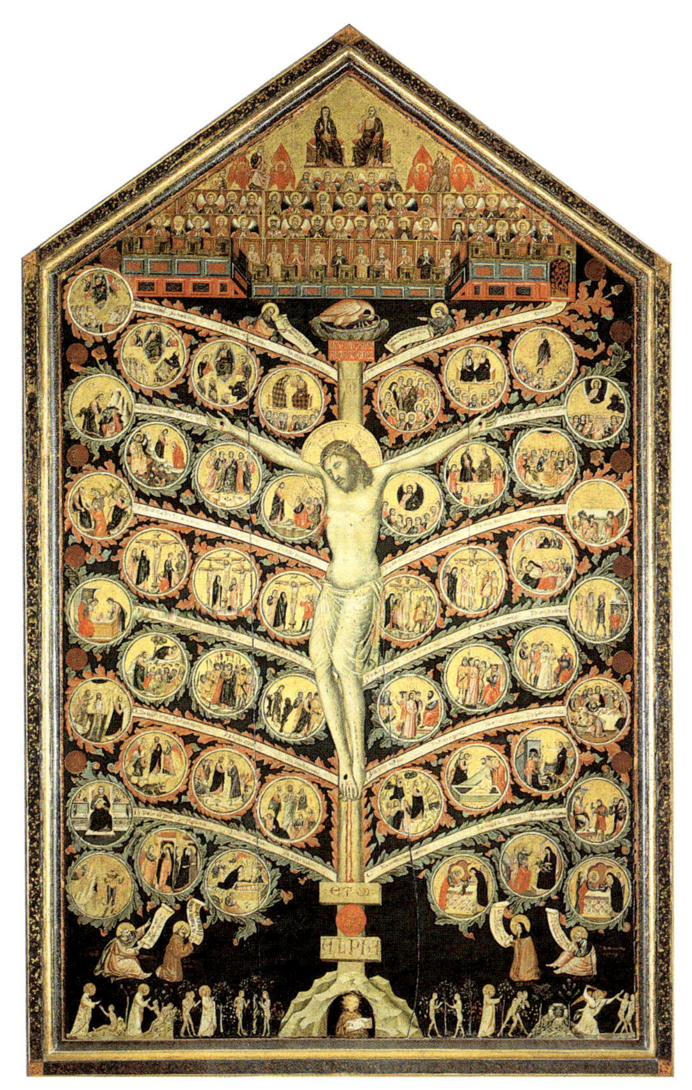

59

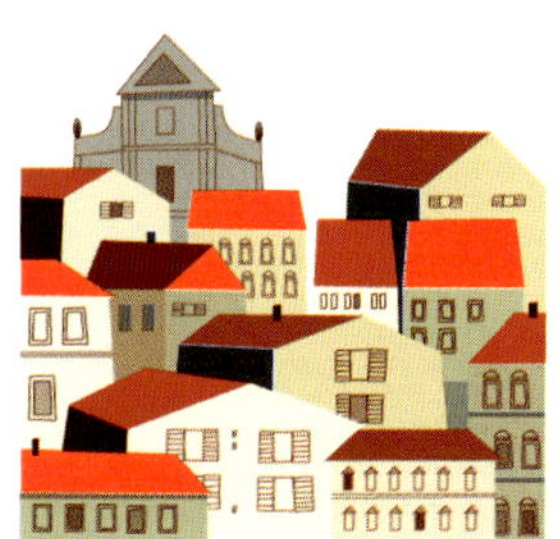

Sale Bizantine

Byzantine Rooms

JACOPO DE CIONE

Stories from the Childhood of Christ, ca 1370

Bethlehem's high, crenellated city walls and turrets serve as the backdrop for the *Slaughter of Innocents*, one of the most poignant episodes in Christ's life. Trying to prevent the coming of the saviour, Herod has all newborn boys killed. But Jesus is already in a faraway grotto, warmed by an ox and donkey, and adored by the Magi Kings. Then, once again in flight, wrapped in the loving, protective arms of his Mother, towards the land of Egypt...

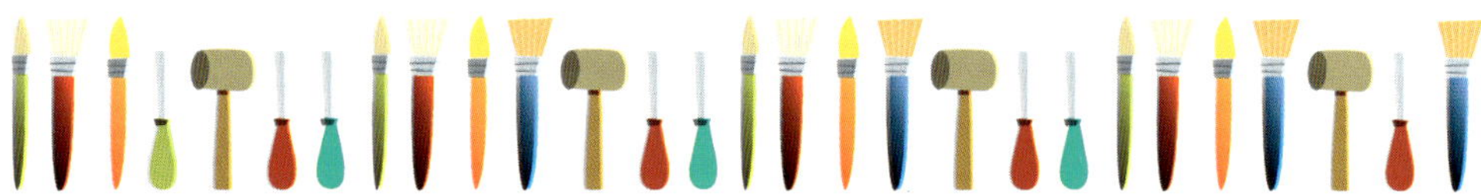

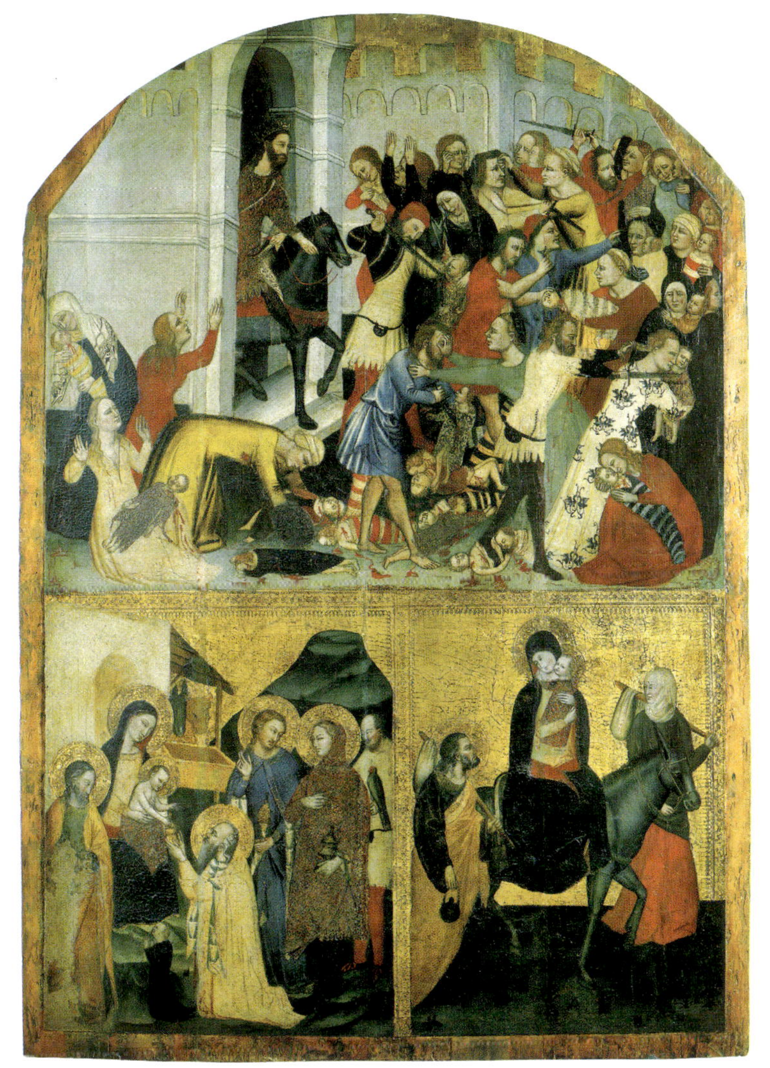

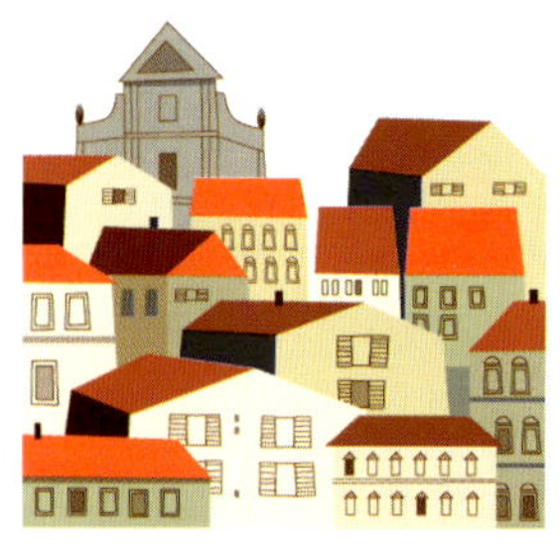

Sale del primo piano

First-floor Rooms

LORENZO MONACO

Annunciation, ca 1418

Held aloft by his great, still open, multi-coloured wings, Gabriel the Archangel, dressed in a streaming coloured mantle, has yet to set foot upon the ground. The Virgin Mary, however, has already seen him and withdraws fearfully, regarding him with some suspicion. This is the story of the *Annunciation*, which unfolds against a dazzling gold background, with four saints looking on at the sides. All the figures are slight and elongated: they seem to have neither weight nor volume.

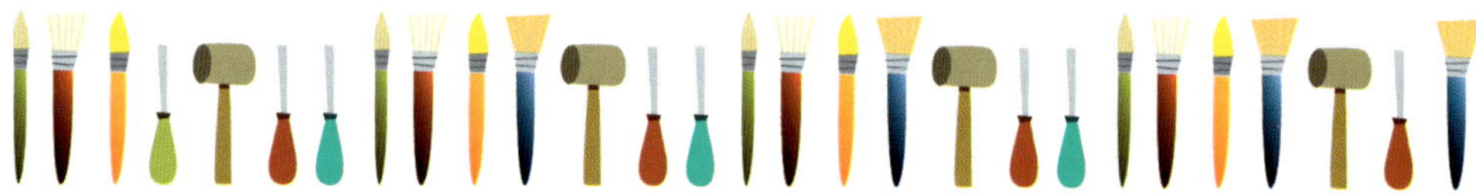

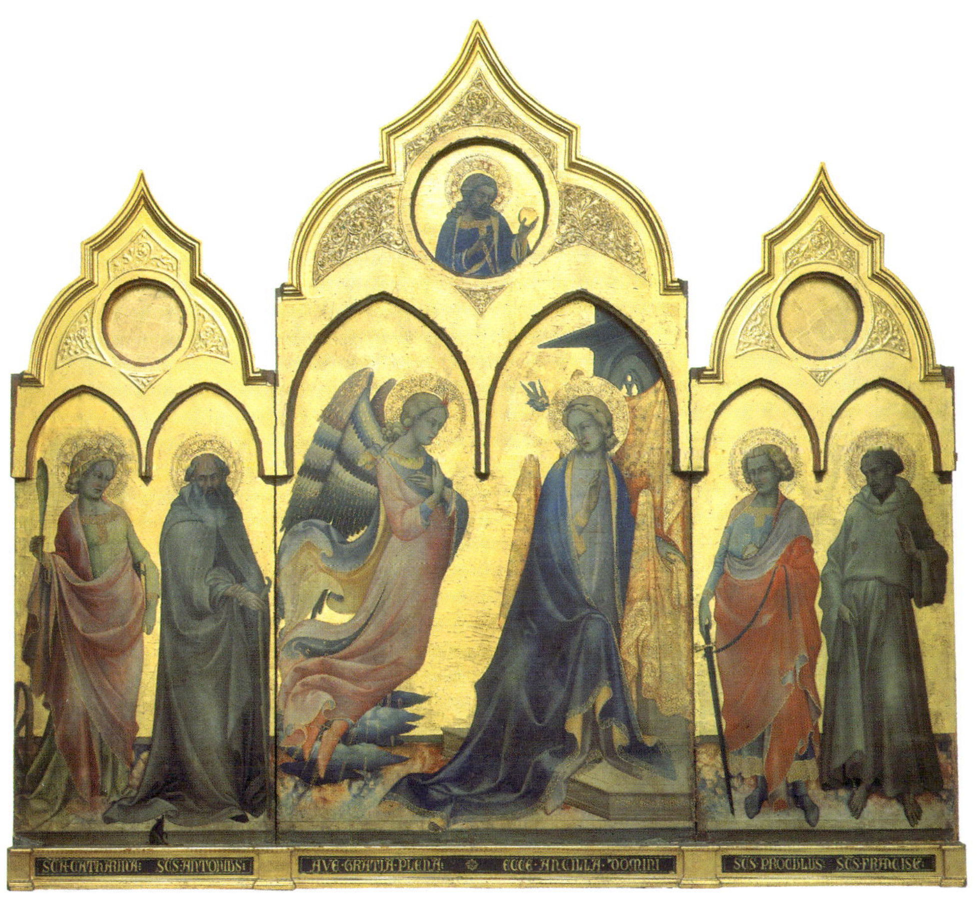
AVE·GRATIA·PLENA:
ECCE·ANCILLA·DOMINI

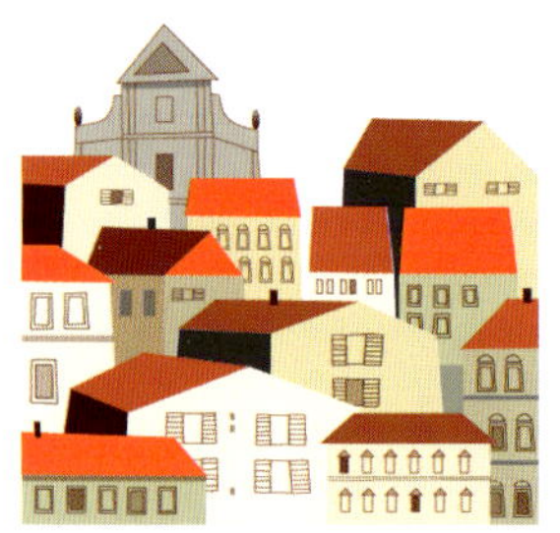

Sale del primo piano

First-floor Rooms

Russian Icons

These belonged to the art collections of the Lorraine grand dukes. They are for the most part small works, suitable as religious articles for private devotion. They moreover serve as important testimony to the collecting passions of the grand dukes, who were curious about everything, and therefore went as far as Russia to enrich their collections. Icons, which are characteristic of the eastern Christian rites, are sacred images painted on wood or, sometimes, glass.

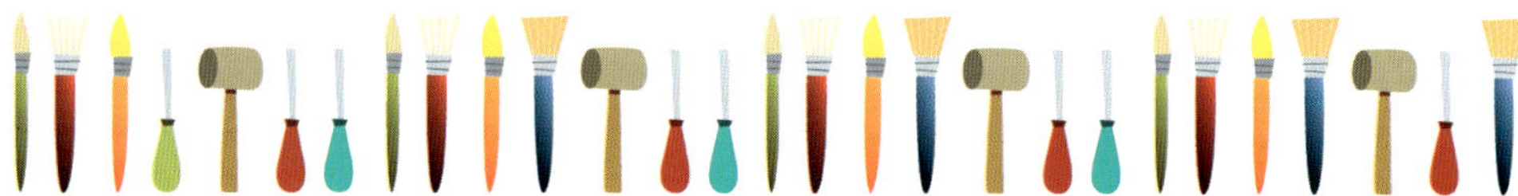

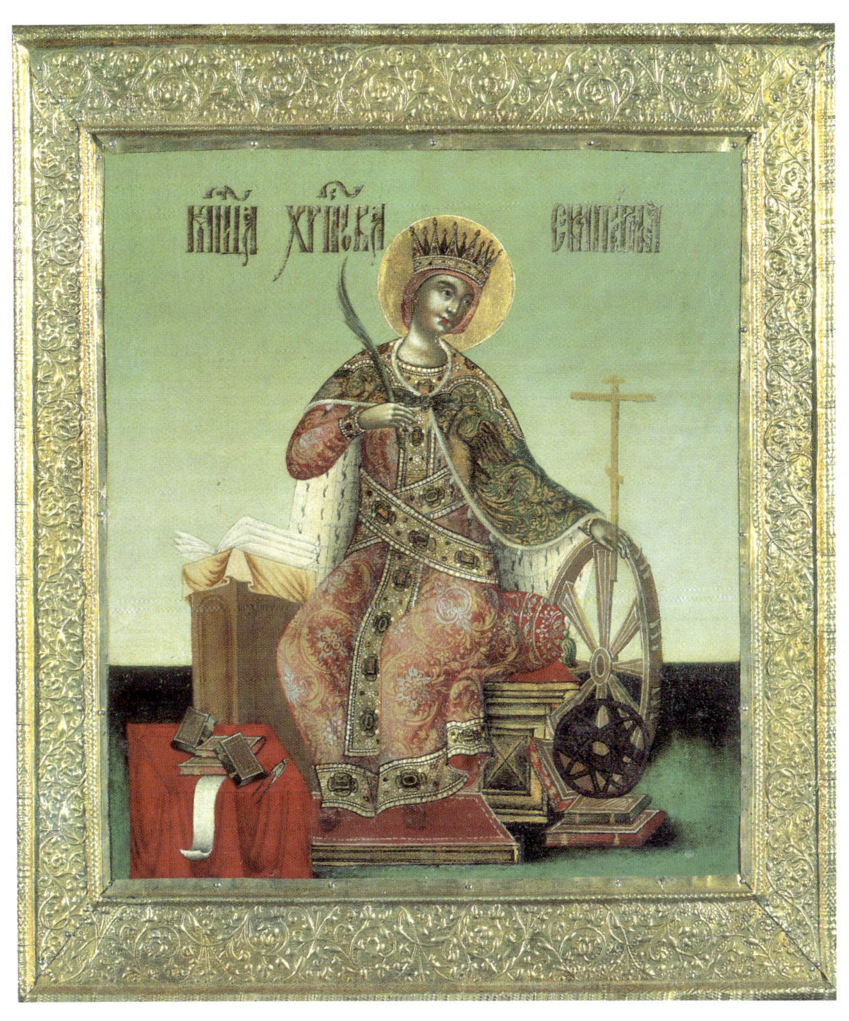

Rusian School, *Saint Catherine*, 18th C.

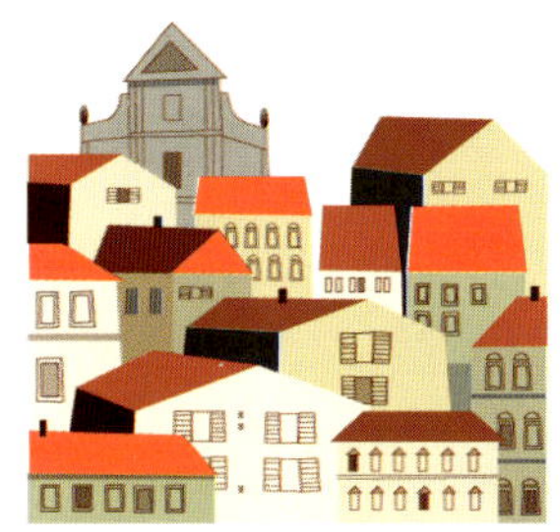

Sale degli Strumenti musicali

Musical Instruments Rooms

The *Luigi Cherubini Conservatory* holds a rich collection of exquisite historical artefacts. Its core is represented by the musical instruments from the collections of the Medici and Lorraine grand dukes, which were once held in Palazzo Pitti. You may ask: what do musical instruments have to do with the Academy and its paintings and sculptures? Well, because originally the Conservatory was part of the Accademia: it represented the school's *second class*, while painting, sculpture and architecture were its *first*…

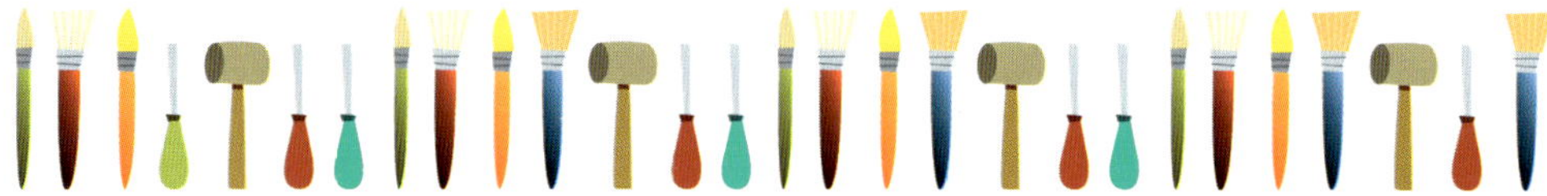

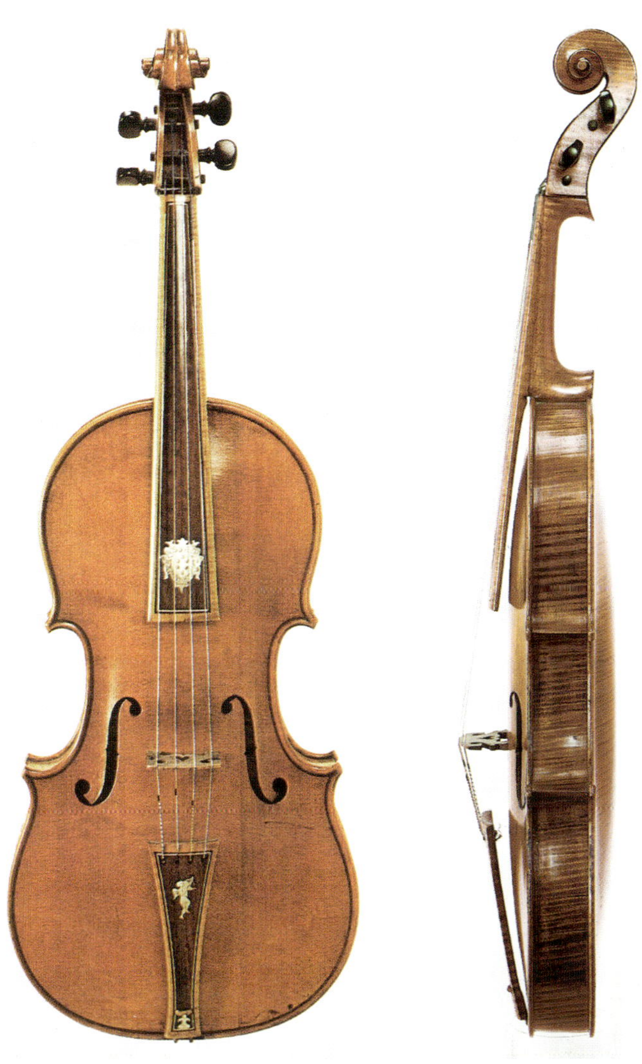

Viola by
Stradivarius,
1690

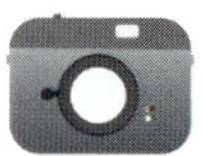 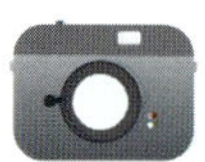 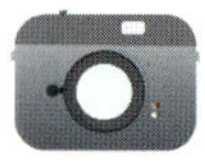 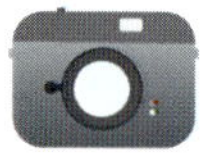 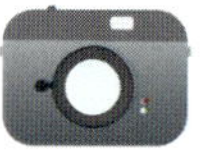 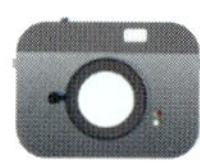 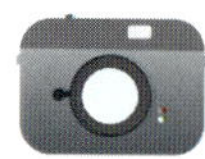

There then, that is the history of Florence's Accademia Gallery and its collections.

Piazza della Signoria today holds a copy the most famous giant in the world: why not go and visit him? And, while you are at it, have a look at the many other masterpieces of Florentine Renaissance sculpture that you will find there...

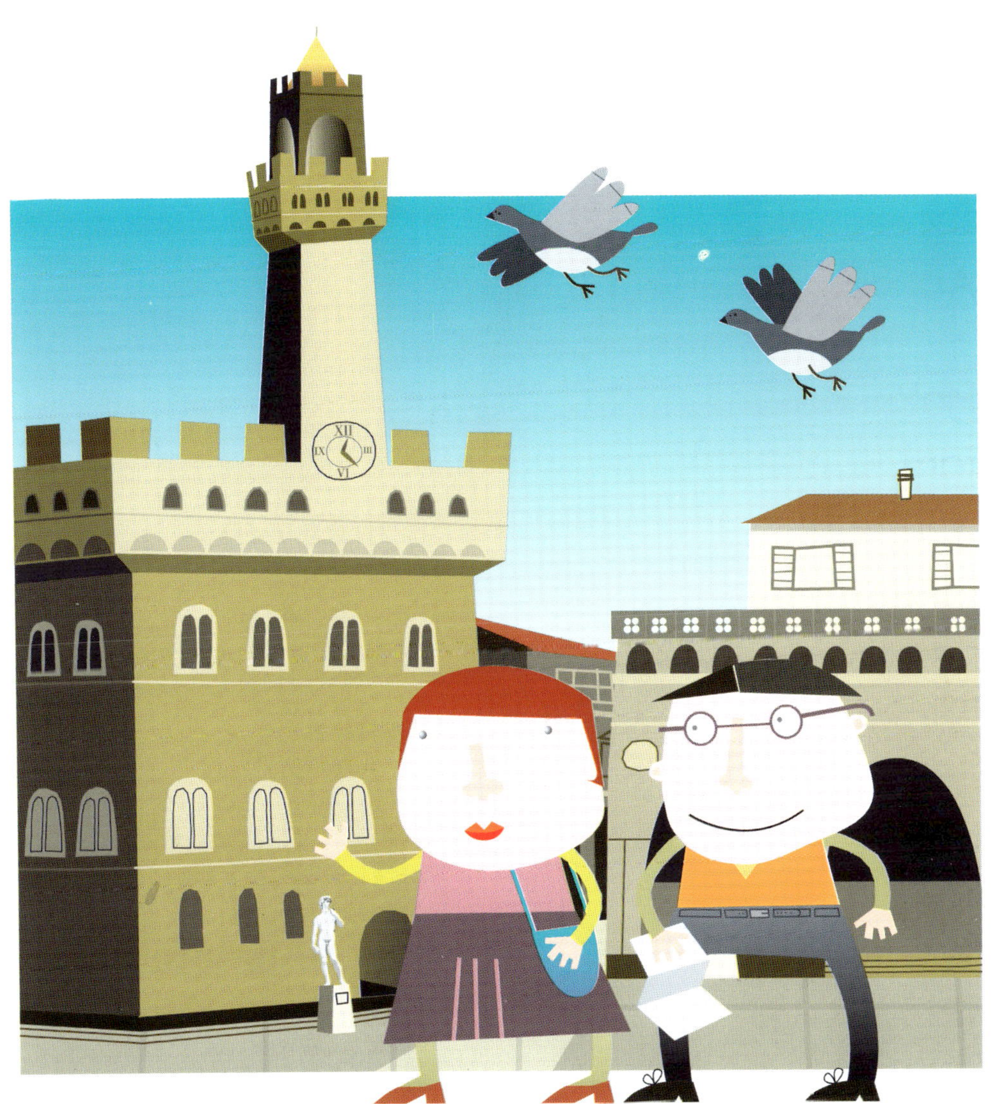

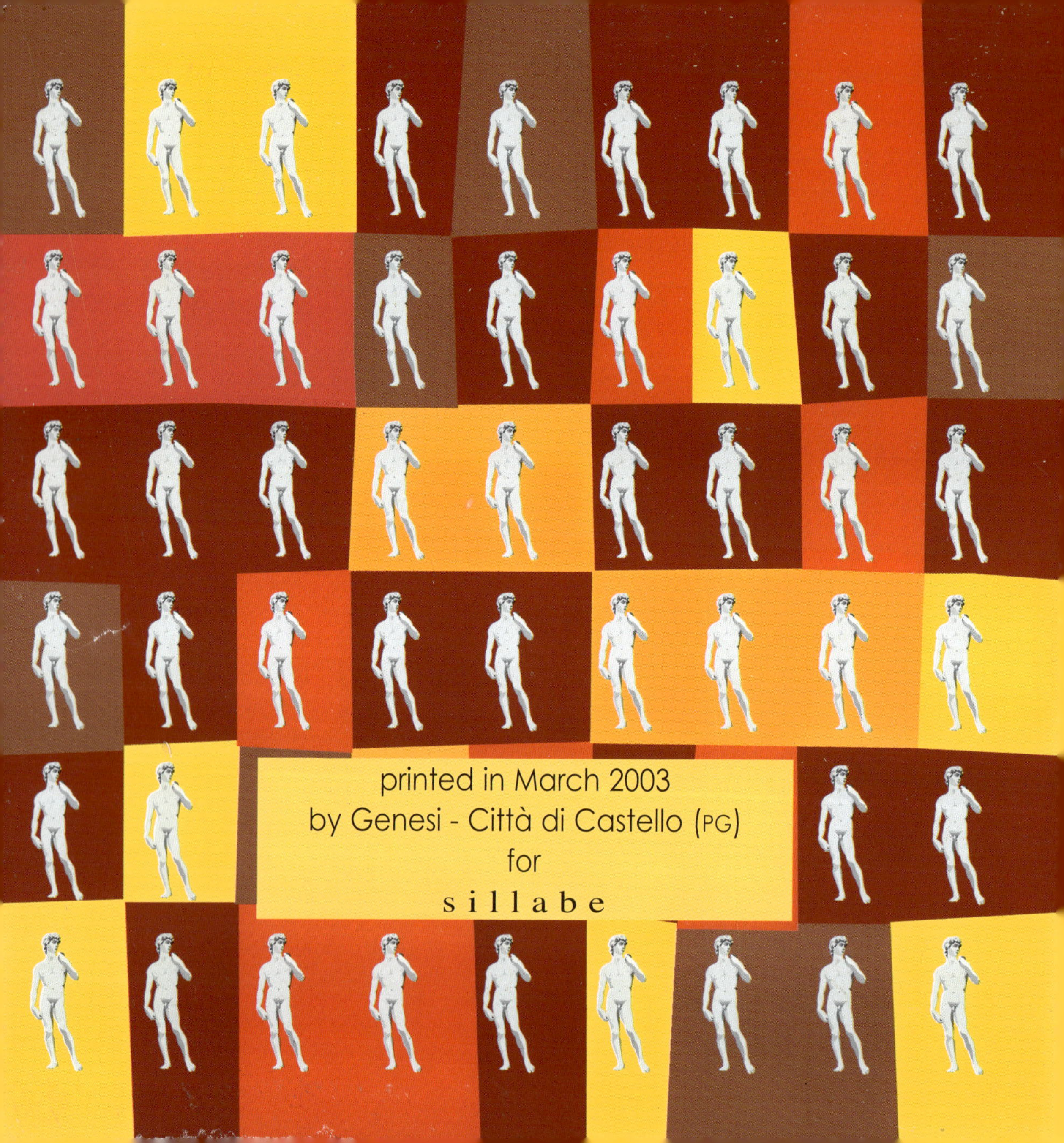
printed in March 2003
by Genesi - Città di Castello (PG)
for
sillabe